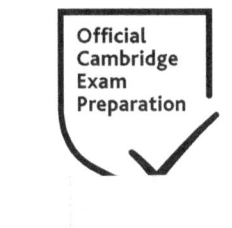

Complete IELTS

Bands 4–5

Workbook *without Answers*

Rawdon Wyatt

Shaftesbury Road, Cambridge CB2 8EA, United Kingdom

One Liberty Plaza, 20th Floor, New York, NY 10006, USA

477 Williamstown Road, Port Melbourne, VIC 3207, Australia

314–321, 3rd Floor, Plot 3, Splendor Forum, Jasola District Centre, New Delhi – 110025, India

103 Penang Road, #05-06/07, Visioncrest Commercial, Singapore 238467

Cambridge University Press & Assessment is a department of the University of Cambridge.

We share the University's mission to contribute to society through the pursuit of education, learning and research at the highest international levels of excellence.

Information on this title: www.cambridge.org/9781009672153

© Cambridge University Press & Assessment 2012

This publication is in copyright. Subject to statutory exception and to the provisions of relevant collective licensing agreements, no reproduction of any part may take place without the written permission of Cambridge University Press & Assessment.

First published 2012
20 19 18 17 16 15 14 13 12 11 10 9 8 7 6 5 4 3 2

Printed in Great Britain by CPI Group (UK) Ltd, Croydon CR0 4YY

A catalogue record for this publication is available from the British Library

ISBN 978-1-009-68362-3 Student's Book with Answers
ISBN 978-1-009-68361-6 Student's Book without Answers
ISBN 978-0-521-18515-8 Teacher's Book
ISBN 978-1-009-67216-0 Workbook with Answers
ISBN 978-1-009-67215-3 Workbook without Answers

Additional resources for this publication at www.cambridge.org/elt/completeielts

Cambridge University Press & Assessment has no responsibility for the persistence or accuracy of URLs for external or third-party internet websites referred to in this publication, and does not guarantee that any content on such websites is, or will remain, accurate or appropriate. Information regarding prices, travel timetables, and other factual information given in this work is correct at the time of first printing but Cambridge University Press & Assessment does not guarantee the accuracy of such information thereafter.

Contents

	Map of the units	4
1	**Great places to be**	6
2	**People's lives**	12
3	**Getting from A to B**	18
4	**It was all new once**	24
5	**Animal world**	30
6	**Being human**	36
7	**Literacy skills**	42
8	**Tourist attractions**	48
9	**Every drop counts**	54
10	**Building design**	60
	Recording scripts	66
	Acknowledgements	75

Map of the units

Unit title	Reading	Listening
1 Great places to be	Reading 1: *The best cities in the world* • Table completion Reading 2: *A city survey with a difference* • Note completion	Listening: Renting an apartment • Form completion
2 People's lives	Reading 1: *Patrick Malone* • Flow-chart completion Reading 2: *Sylvia Earle, Underwater hero* • Short-answer questions • True / False / Not Given	Listening: Preparing for a magazine interview • Predicting the answers • Note completion
3 Getting from A to B	Reading 1: *The Boeing 787* • Labelling a diagram Reading 2: *Pedestrians only* • Matching headings	Listening: Information about a train journey • Labelling a diagram • Multiple choice • Listening for synonyms and paraphrases
4 It was all new once	Reading 1: *The ballpoint pen* • Multiple choice Reading 2: *Marcel Bich* • Summary completion	Listening: Market research interview • Sentence completion • Pick from a list
5 Animal world	Reading 1: *The honey badger* • Sentence completion Reading 2: *On the trail of the honey badger* • Pick from a list	Listening: Information about a college event • Table completion • Labelling a plan
6 Being human	Reading 1: *Breaking the habit* • Yes / No / Not Given Reading 2: *Fighting fear using virtual reality* • Summary completion with a box	Listening: Things that make people happy • Matching • Pick from a list
7 Literacy skills	Reading: *Graphic novels* • Matching information • Table completion	Listening: Applying for tickets to a book fair • Form completion • Multiple choice
8 Tourist attractions	Reading: *Holidays with a difference* • Summary completion • Matching features	Listening: Tour guide giving information • Sentence completion • Table completion
9 Every drop counts	Reading: *The rain makers* • Matching headings • Sentence completion • Pick from a list	Listening: A tutor and a student talking about an essay • Matching • Flow-chart completion
10 Building design	Reading: *The man who tried to destroy Paris* • Multiple choice • Matching sentence endings • Yes / No / Not Given	Listening: A talk on the Beijing Olympic stadium • Note completion

Writing	Vocabulary and Spelling	Grammar
Writing Task 1 • Describing pie charts and bar charts • Selecting key features • Using accurate data	• Collocations and prepositional phrases • Key vocabulary • Spelling: Making nouns plural	Present simple and present continuous
Writing Task 2 • Analysing the task • Planning an answer • Writing an introduction • Using linkers: *also*, *and*, *but* and *however*	• Working out the meanings of words • Key vocabulary • Spelling: Changes when adding *–ed*	Past simple
Writing Task 1 • Describing tables and charts • Comparing data and selecting key points • Writing in paragraphs	• *make* and *cause* • Key vocabulary • Spelling: Changes when adding *–er* and *–est* to adjectives	Making comparisons with adjectives and adverbs
Writing Task 2 • To what extent do you agree or disagree? • Brainstorming ideas • Organising your ideas	• What type of word is it? 1 • Key vocabulary • Spelling: Using and misusing double letters	Present perfect
Writing Task 1 • Summarising two charts • Comparing bar charts • Grouping information	• What type of word is it? 2 • Prepositions in time phrases • Words that give directions • Key vocabulary • Spelling: Small words often misspelled	Countable and uncountable nouns
Writing Task 2 • Answering a single question • Planning an answer	• Word building • Key vocabulary • Spelling: Suffixes	Zero and first conditionals (*if/ unless*)
Writing Task 1 • Describing trends • Using verb and noun phrases • Writing an overview	• *raise* or *rise*? • Key vocabulary • Spelling: Forming adverbs from adjectives	Prepositions to describe graphs
Writing Task 2 • Answering two questions • Analysing the task • Writing a conclusion	• *tourism* or *tourist*? • Key vocabulary • Spelling: Introductory and linking phrases	Relative pronouns: *who*, *which*, *that*, *where*
Writing Task 1 • Summarising a diagram • Planning an answer • Ordering the information • Comparing two diagrams	• *effect*, *benefit*, *advantage*, *disadvantage* • Key vocabulary • Spelling: Some common mistakes	The passive Sequencers
Writing Task 2 • Discussing opposing views and giving your opinion • Analysing the task and brainstorming ideas • Structuring an answer • Proofing an answer for spelling and punctuation mistakes	• Word choice • Guessing the meaning of words • Improving vocabulary use • Key vocabulary • Spelling: Proofing your essay for common spelling mistakes	Modal verbs

Unit 1 Great places to be

Reading 1
Table completion

1 You are going to read a passage about some of the cities above. Read the passage quickly and answer these questions.

1 Which of the cities above are mentioned?
....

2 How many advantages are given for each city? ....

2 Find words or phrases in the passage which have a similar meaning to the underlined words and phrases in the table below.

well-known: *famous*   quality of life: ....
excellent: ....   most pleasant: ....
very: ....   not many: ....
residents: ....   a lot: ....

3 Now complete the table. Choose ONE word from the passage for each answer.

The best cities in the world

In a recent internet survey, tourists and business travellers were asked to rate 50 cities around the world, from the best to the worst. Of the top three cities, two were in Europe and one was in Australia.

In third place was London, scoring highly mainly because it was the most famous city on the list of 50 surveyed. It was also seen as a very good place to do business, and was an important cultural centre. However, it lost points because people believed it was an extremely expensive place to live.

Sydney was also a very popular destination, achieving second place on the list because people believed it had the friendliest inhabitants, as well as the best standard of living and the nicest climate. It failed to make the top spot, however, because people thought there were very few things to see there, and many also thought it was too far away from other business and cultural centres.

At the top of the list was Paris. Despite problems such as the large amount of traffic, it beat other cities to first place because people considered it to be the most interesting city, with more museums, art galleries and places of interest than anywhere else. People also thought it was the best city to take a holiday in.

City	Overall position in survey	Perceived advantages	Perceived disadvantages
London	1	• Is more <u>well-known</u> than the other cities. • Has <u>excellent</u> 2 .... opportunities.	Is <u>very</u> 3 ....
Sydney	Second	• <u>Residents</u> are the 4 .... • Has the best <u>quality of life</u>. • Has the <u>most pleasant</u> 5	<u>Not many</u> things to see.
Paris	6	• Is more 7 .... than other cities.	Has <u>a lot</u> of 8 ....

Reading 2
Note completion

4 You are going to read a passage about a type of city survey. Read the passage quickly and answer these questions.

1 What do 'best city' websites usually show?
....

2 What does the CBI ask people to do?
....

5 Match the words or phrases (1–7), which are underlined in the passage, with the words or phrases (a–g) which have a similar meaning.

1	similar to	a	a number of
2	each	b	every
3	total	c	get a job
4	several	d	helpful
5	useful	e	like
6	find work	f	local
7	regional	g	maximum

6 Now complete the notes below. Choose ONE WORD OR A NUMBER from the passage for each answer.

The City Brands Index

The CBI believes that cities are like **1** .... which people can buy when they go shopping.

Surveys take place every **2** ....

A maximum of **3** .... cities are included in the survey.

A number of different **4** .... are included in the survey.

The CBI list is helpful for:

- people who are trying to decide where to **5** .... or get a job.
- people who are looking for a good **6** .... destination.
- local **7** .... who want to make their city a better place.

A city survey with a difference

There are many websites on the Internet which provide lists of the world's best cities to visit, live or work in. These lists usually grade the cities in order, from 'best' to 'worst', and are based on facts and figures provided by local or national organisations.

The City Brands Index (CBI) also provides a list of best and worst cities. However, unlike other surveys, it is based on the idea that cities are <u>similar to</u> products in shops. It asks ordinary people in other countries to grade cities in the same way that they would grade a product, like a soft drink or a car. What is particularly different about the CBI is that the people who take part in the survey may not have ever visited the cities. Instead, they are asked to say what they think the cities are like, basing their opinions on things like news stories, magazine articles or television programmes they have heard or seen.

<u>Each</u> year, about 10,000 people in 20 countries take part in the CBI survey, and they grade a <u>total</u> of 50 cities. They do this by filling in an online questionnaire. There are <u>several</u> categories in the survey. These include things like the economy, education, the environment, local culture, climate and what the city's residents are like.

The CBI list is <u>useful</u> because it helps people choose a good place to live, <u>find work</u> or take a holiday. It also helps <u>regional</u> governments to understand why people and businesses are, or are not, coming to their cities, and so shows them areas which they could develop or improve.

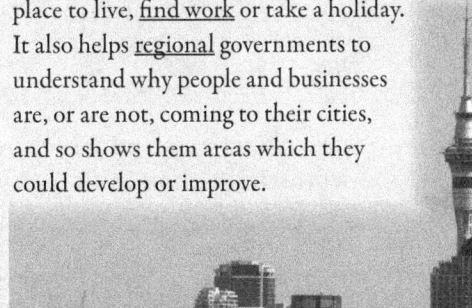

Great places to be

Listening
Form completion

❶ (02) **Listen to four short conversations, and complete these sentences by choosing the correct word and/or number.**

1 The man is moving house on Friday *3rd / 13th / 30th*.
2 The man has come from *Crawford / Crauford / Crawsord*.
3 The man's mobile number is *0780 29227 / 0872 92702 / 0870 292720*.
4 Sue lives at *70 Sydney / 70 Sidney / 17 Sydney* Avenue.

❷ (03) **Now listen to these short conversations, and complete the sentences with no more than TWO WORDS AND/OR A NUMBER.**

1 The woman's name is ....
2 The woman's mobile number is ....
3 The man's address is ...., Fenton.
4 The woman arrived on .... April.

❸ **You are going to hear a woman calling an accommodation agency about an apartment she wants to rent. Before you listen, look at the form on the right and answer the following questions.**

In which gaps do you think you will need to write:
a a word (or words) only? ....
b a number only? ....
c a word (or words) and a number? ....

❹ (04) **Now listen and complete the form. Write no more than TWO WORDS AND/OR A NUMBER for each answer.**

Good Moves Accommodation Agency

Call taken by: *Ben*

Name: **1** ....

Telephone: **2** ....

Heard about us from: **3** ....

Type of accommodation preferred:
4 ....

Number of people: **5** ....

Preferred location: Wants to be close to
6 ....

Price: maximum **7** £ .... per person
(including **8** ....)

Additional notes:

I suggested Flat 3 at **9** .... Road in Bampton.

I will send further details to customer by
10 ....

Vocabulary
Collocations and prepositional phrases

❶ **Which of these words are adjectives, and which are nouns? Write the words in the box in the correct columns.**

festivals   friendly   food   tasty   inhabitants
lively   pretty   scenery   spectacular   villages

Adjectives	Nouns
friendly	festivals

Unit 1

2 Complete the gaps in this passage with an adjective and noun pair from Exercise 1.

My home city (Part 1)

What can I tell you about my home city? First of all, I must mention its **1** _friendly inhabitants_. Everyone smiles and says hello when you meet them. Then there's the **2** .... which you can get everywhere. It's delicious, and really cheap. Four or five times a year there are **3** .... where people celebrate important events with street parties and other fun events. And if you get fed up with the city, you can get a bus into the countryside, where there are lots of **4** .... The hills and mountains there also provide some really **5** ....

3 Which of these words are adjectives, and which are nouns? Write the words in the box in the correct columns.

| ~~apartments~~ | ~~crowded~~ | city | industrial |
| lifestyle | relaxed | streets | tiny |

Adjectives	Nouns
crowded	apartments

4 Complete each gap in the passage below with TWO words from Exercise 3.

My home city (Part 2)

It has its bad points as well. It's an **1** ...., which means that there is a lot of pollution, and there are also lots of ugly factories everywhere. Most people live in **2** .... because houses are too expensive. They work really hard, and they can't afford to enjoy the sort of **3** .... that many people associate with my country. And it can take ages to walk along the **4** .... in the city centre because there are so many people and so much traffic.

5 Complete these sentences by choosing the best preposition.

1 My house is _by_ / _in_ the sea. You walk out of the front door straight onto the beach.
2 I live in a two-room flat _in_ / _on_ the outskirts of the city.
3 We spent two weeks in a small village _in_ / _on_ the mountains.
4 Property prices _by_ / _in_ the city centre are so expensive that only a few people can afford them.
5 The town of Wadi Musa is _near_ / _on_ the desert. It's only an hour's drive away.
6 I would hate to live _by_ / _in_ the country. It must be so quiet and boring there.
7 When I was a growing up in the UK, I lived _in_ / _on_ the suburbs.
8 Our house was right _by_ / _near_ a river. There was even a place at the end of garden where you could leave your boat.

Key vocabulary

6 Complete the passage with words from the box.

conclude	crime	diverse	impact
industrial	influence	lifestyle	locals
ranks	reaction	~~reputation~~	surround

The city where I live has a bad **1** _reputation_ because of its high **2** .... rate. If you believe everything you read in the newspapers, you might **3** .... that everyone who visits the city has their wallet stolen or gets attacked in the street the moment they arrive. In recent years this has had a negative **4** .... on the number of tourists who come to the city, since news stories can really **5** .... people when they are thinking of visiting a place. I won't pretend that my city is the best place in the world. It's noisy and crowded, and ugly **6** .... estates **7** .... it on all sides. In fact, it **8** .... as sixth on a national list of the country's worst places to live, and for most visitors, their first **9** .... is 'Oh no, what a horrible place!' However, I think this is unfair. There are some attractive old buildings in the city, the **10** .... population gives the place a colourful, international feel, most of the **11** .... are friendly and welcoming, and because prices are low, people can afford to enjoy a **12** .... that is considerably better than in many other cities.

Great places to be 9

Grammar

Present simple and present continuous

1 Each of these sentences contains a mistake. Cross out the mistake and write the correct word or words at the end of the sentence.

1 Living in the countryside ~~is having~~ many advantages. ..has..

2 I'm feeling that cities are dirty, noisy and expensive places. ....

3 Winters in my city are hard because it's snowing a lot. ....

4 City life becoming more and more expensive. ....

5 I'm study English at a language school in my home town. ....

6 People generally are believing that country life is healthier than city life. ....

7 The city council is build lots of new apartment blocks in the suburbs. ....

8 I'm not liking small towns because there's nothing to do. ....

2 Complete the passage with the correct form of the verbs in the box (present simple or present continuous).

| be (x3) | become | have (x2) | like | ~~live~~ | look |
| meet | play | rise | sit | stay | think | watch |

I 1 ..live.. in Buenos Aires, the capital of Argentina. I 2 .... a small flat in the suburbs, but at the moment I 3 .... with my parents in the city centre because my mother 4 .... ill and I 5 .... after her until she gets better.

I 6 .... that Buenos Aires is a really lively and exciting city, and I 7 .... it here a lot. City life in general 8 .... lots of advantages. There 9 .... always so many things to see and do.

One of the things I enjoy the most is something called 'people watching'. So right now I 10 .... on my parents' balcony and 11 .... people in the street below.

In the evenings I 12 .... my friends for a meal, or sometimes we 13 .... volleyball in one of the city parks. Of course, there 14 .... bad sides to the city as well. It 15 .... more and more crowded, for example, and the crime rate 16 .... because there are a lot of people out of work.

Writing

Task 1

1 Look at the pie chart and match sentence parts 1–7 with a–g.

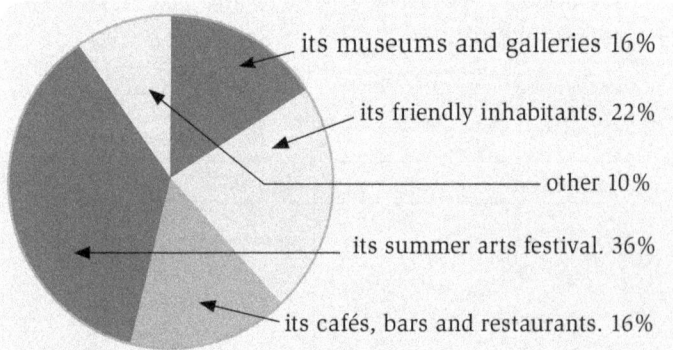

Edinburgh visitors survey: What are the city's best features?

1 The chart shows
2 The largest percentage, 36 percent,
3 22 percent
4 16 percent of visitors
5 The city's cafés, bars and restaurants were popular with
6 10 percent
7 Overall, the majority of visitors

a choose its museums and galleries as the things they like the most.
b choose its friendly inhabitants.
c choose other things.
d think that its summer arts festival is the best thing about it.
e think the city's cultural attractions are its best features.
f another 16 percent of visitors.
g what visitors to Edinburgh like most about the city.

❷ Now look at the chart about where tourists stay at a holiday destination. Put the sentences below in the correct order to make a summary.

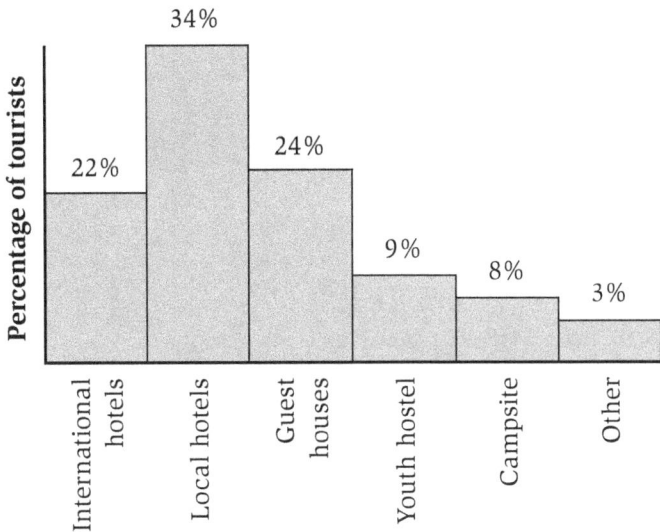

Where tourists stay at Casuarina Beach

A 24 percent of tourists stay in these. ....

B The youth hostel and the campsite accommodate nine percent and eight percent of tourists. ....

C Overall, more visitors stay in hotels than in any other kind of accommodation. ....

D The largest percentage, 34 percent, stay in the town's local hotels. ....

E The chart gives information about the different types of accommodation that tourists stay in when they visit Casuarina Beach. ....1......

F International hotels are also popular, with 22 percent of tourists choosing to stay in one. ....

G A further three percent stay in other types of accommodation. ....

H Guest houses are the next most popular type of accommodation. ....

Spelling
Making nouns plural

❶ Write the singular and plural forms of the words from the box in the table.

| boss | ~~boy~~ | foot | man | match |
| party | potato | visitor | wife | |

Rule	Singular	Plural
1 Add s	boy	boys
2 Add es		
3 Change one or more of the letters		
4 Change the last letter to i and add es		
5 Remove the last two letters and add ves		

❷ These sentences contain a singular word that should be plural. Each word follows one of the rules in the table above. <u>Underline</u> the word, then write the plural form at the end of each sentence.

1 There are three really good <u>beach</u> a few miles from my home. *beaches*

2 Many people grow their own peas, beans and tomato. ....

3 Everyone knows that sugar is bad for your tooth. ....

4 There are more woman in the government now than there used to be. ....

5 He told us some really funny story about the time he worked on a farm. ....

6 I'm staying with my brother for a few day. ....

7 In my country, it is illegal to carry knife in the street. ....

8 Bus into town run every 30 minutes during the day. ....

9 There are several good hotel in my town. ....

10 My cat is always bringing dead mouse into my flat. ....

Great places to be 11

Unit 2 People's lives

Reading 1
Flow-chart completion

❶ You are going to read about a traveller and explorer called Patrick Malone. Look at the flow chart. What type of information do you think you need for each gap?

1	4
2	5
3	6

Patrick Malone

Born in Switzerland in 1968.

↓

Moved to **1** .... when he was twelve.

↓

Studied **2** .... at university.

↓

Got a job as a **3** ....

↓

Once travelled more than **4** .... on foot on a single trip.

↓

Often went walking in places that were quite **5** ....

↓

Joined an **6** .... to the Amazon.

❷ Use the words in the box to complete the flow chart above and then check your answers by reading the passage.

| Britain | expedition | Human Geography |
| 1,400 kilometres | remote | teacher |

Patrick Malone (Part 1)

Patrick Malone is a traveller, writer and broadcaster. He was born in 1968 in Basel, Switzerland, where his British parents were working for a pharmaceutical company. His family left Switzerland when he was twelve, and returned to their home in Britain. For the next six years, Malone attended the local secondary school. He then went to Leeds University to do a course in Human Geography. He wanted to become a town planner. However, the only work he could find was as a teacher at a local school.

During his holidays and free time, he went walking, often covering very long distances very quickly. On one occasion he walked the entire length of Britain, a distance of over 1,400 kilometres, in less than a month. He enjoyed the experience and the challenge so much that he started walking in different parts of the world, usually in fairly remote areas away from major population centres. The people he met and the experiences he had on these trips provided him with some excellent material for his classes.

It was during one trip that he met his old university tutor, Don Perkins. At the time, Perkins was putting together a team of geographers and biologists for a research trip to the Amazon, and asked Malone if he would like to go with them. The expedition was for a whole year, and so he had to give up his job at the school, but Malone did not hesitate to accept Perkins' offer. He sold his car to make some money, bought an airline ticket for Brazil and set off.

12 Unit 2

❸ Read the next part of the passage, and complete gaps 7–12. Choose NO MORE THAN TWO WORDS AND/OR A NUMBER for each one.

Patrick Malone (Part 2)

The Amazon expedition, which took six months and covered a distance of almost 2,500 kilometres, was a great success. The group discovered some new plant and insect species, as well as a forest tribe which people had never heard of. Malone enjoyed the trip so much that he decided to become a full-time explorer. He earned money by writing travel articles for magazines and newspapers, which he illustrated with his own photographs.

In 1996, he married Margaret Logan, an American doctor he had met while travelling around Africa. In 1998 they had Adam, the first of three children (twins Amelia and Jennifer were born a year later). Many families at this stage would settle down, but Margaret and Patrick decided to keep travelling, spending two years walking around India and another twelve months exploring the islands of Indonesia.

When they returned home, they wrote a magazine article about travelling with small children. It was so popular that they were asked to write several more articles on the same subject. This was followed by an offer from a television company to present a TV series about travelling with children. The series ran for 12 years, and won several television awards. Today they still make the most of every opportunity to travel, and have recently returned from the South Pacific.

Travelled 2,500 kilometres through the Amazon.

↓

7 .... a tribe that nobody knew existed.

↓

8 .... someone he met on a trip.

↓

They had 9 ....: Adam, Amelia and Jennifer.

↓

Explored the Indonesian islands for 10 ....

↓

Made a successful 11 ....

↓

Still likes to 12 .... whenever possible.

Reading 2
Short-answer questions; True / False / Not Given

❹ Look at this picture and answer the questions below.

1 What do you think this person does?
   ....

2 What are the dangers involved in a job like this?
   ....
   ....
   ....

❺ You are going to read a passage about a woman called Sylvia Earle. Before you read the passage, look at the title and the subheading. What do you think the passage will talk about?

a a woman who has an interesting hobby
b a scientist who wants to know more about the sea
c a student who wants to become an underwater explorer

❻ Read the passage on page 14. Choose NO MORE THAN TWO WORDS AND/OR A NUMBER FROM THE PASSAGE for each answer.

1 What career did Sylvia decide to follow after her first dive? ....

2 How far under water did she go in order to break a world record? ....

3 What was causing harm to everything living in the sea? ....

4 Where does Sylvia think we should get our fish from? ....

People's lives

Sylvia Earle, underwater hero

She has spent her working life studying the world's oceans

Sylvia Earle is an underwater explorer and marine biologist who was born in the USA in 1935. She became interested in the world's oceans from an early age. As a child, she liked to stand on the beach for hours and look at the sea, wondering what it must be like under the surface.

When she was 16, she finally got a chance to make her first dive. It was this dive that inspired her to become an underwater explorer. Since then, she has spent more than 6,500 hours under water, and has led more than seventy expeditions worldwide. She has also made the deepest dive ever, reaching a record-breaking depth of 381 metres.

In 1970, she became famous around the world when she became the captain of the first all-female team to live under water. The team spent two weeks in an underwater 'house'. The research they carried out showed the damage that pollution was causing to marine life, and especially to coral reefs. Her team also studied the problem of over-fishing. Fishing methods meant that people were catching too many fish, Earle warned, and many species were in danger of becoming extinct.

Since then she has written several books and magazine articles in which she suggests ways of reducing the damage that is being done to the world's oceans. One way, she believes, is to rely on fish farms for seafood, and reduce the amount of fishing that is done out at sea. Although she no longer eats seafood herself, she realises the importance it plays in our diets. It would be wrong to tell people they should stop eating fish from the sea, she says. However, they need to reduce the impact they are having on the ocean's supplies.

❼ Now decide if these statements are TRUE, FALSE or NOT GIVEN according to the information in the passage.

1. Sylvia Earle lives in the USA. ....
2. Until 1970, nobody had lived underwater before. ....
3. Sylvia Earle was worried about the amount of fish that were being caught. ....
4. Her books offer some solutions to marine problems. ....
5. She thinks people should avoid eating seafood. ....

Listening

Note completion

❶ Look at the notes below. Which answers need:

a words only? ....   b numbers only? ....
c words and numbers? ....

1. First name: ....Toby........   Surname: ....
2. Address: .... Street, Wokingham, Berkshire
3. Date of birth: 5th April ....
4. Telephone: ....
5. Occupation: ....
6. Distance from home to workplace: ....
7. Method of transport to work: ....
8. Free-time activities: cooking, ... travel

❷ (05) Listen to the eight questions, A–H. Match the questions with the notes above.

A = ..4.. B = ... C = ... D = ... E = ...
F = ... G = ... H = ...

❸ (06) Listen to the questions and answers in their correct order. Complete the notes in Exercise 1.

❹ You are going to hear a conversation between Eddie and Bridget about someone that Eddie is going to interview for a magazine. Think about the type of information you need for each space.

❺ (07) Listen to the conversation and complete the notes. Write NO MORE THAN TWO WORDS AND/OR A NUMBER for each answer.

Magazine interview

Name: ...Tom... **1** ....
Occupation: **2** ....
Has written **3** ....
Crossed Gobi desert in **4** ....
Title of latest book: 'Has Anyone Seen **5** .... ?'
Has won 'Travel Book of **6** .... ' award.
Date of interview: Friday **7** ....
Contact number: **8** .... (call to arrange time)
Place of interview: **9** .... , Summertown
See his **10** .... for more information.

Unit 2

Grammar

Past simple

1 Complete the crossword with the past simple forms of these verbs. Refer to the reading passages if you need help.

Across (→):
1 win 2 have 4 buy 5 sell 8 be 10 meet 11 take

Down (↓):
1 go 3 do 4 become 5 spend 6 write 7 leave 9 get

2 Complete this passage with the past simple of the verbs in the box.

be	decide	discover	do	enjoy	go
have	leave	meet	spend	start	win

After I **1** _left_ school, I **2** .... nine months travelling around South-East Asia. I **3** .... to Indonesia, Malaysia, Thailand and Vietnam. I **4** .... lots of different people, **5** .... some great experiences, and **6** .... some fascinating places. I **7** .... it all so much that I **8** .... to work in the travel business. So, I **9** .... a course in Travel and Tourism at my local college. I then **10** .... my own internet travel agency, selling cheap airline tickets. It **11** .... very successful, and today thousands of people use it to buy their tickets and holidays. Last year it **12** .... an award for services to the travel industry.

Vocabulary

Working out the meanings of words

1 Match the first part of each sentence (1–5) with the second part (a–e).

1 *ant*, *ist* and *er* are often used at the end of a word
2 *un* is often used at the beginning of a word
3 *able* and *ic* are often used at the end of a word
4 *re* is often used at the beginning of a word
5 *fy* is often used at the end of a word

a to indicate that something must be done again.
b to change a verb or noun into an adjective.
c to indicate a person, especially a person with a particular job.
d to change a noun or adjective into a verb.
e to make a word negative.

2 Complete these sentences with the correct form of the words in the box.

accept	account	afford	apology	certainty
prefer	run	~~write~~	receive	identity

1 My essay on famous explorers was so bad that I had to ..._rewrite_... it.
2 When you arrive at the hotel, the .... will give you your key and tell you which room you're in.
3 Sylvia Earle thinks that the amount of fish we are catching at sea is ....
4 There were over 300 .... in the race.
5 In my opinion, travelling with friends is .... to travelling on your own.
6 Can you .... the famous explorer in this picture? I think I recognise him, but I'm not sure.
7 Unfortunately, there's a lot of .... about her future with the company, and she may lose her job.
8 This restaurant is not expensive. The food is good and ....
9 She was very .... about missing the meeting and said sorry to everyone.
10 We need a good .... to take care of our business finances.

People's lives

3 Complete these sentences with the correct form of the word in brackets, using the rules in Exercise 1.

1 Unfortunately, the computer I tried to order on the Internet was ...unavailable... (available).
2 He gave me a horrible look. He absolutely .... (terror) me.
3 A sportsman or sportswoman needs a good .... (train) to help them succeed.
4 I can't see you tonight, so can we .... (arrange) our meeting for another time?
5 The audience applauded as the world-famous .... (piano) walked onto the stage.
6 I can't eat seafood because I'm .... (allergy) to it.
7 There were almost 100 .... (apply) for the job.
8 *Dog*, *man*, *flower* and *book* are examples of .... (count) nouns. *Rice*, *water*, *air* and *earth* are .... (count).

Key vocabulary

4 Complete the passage with words and phrases from the box.

account   combines
commentary   community
eventually   prove
regard   voyage

Many people 1 ...regard... Paul Theroux as one of the world's best travel writers. *The Happy Isles of Oceania*, one of his classic travel books, is an 2 .... of a long 3 .... around the islands of the South Pacific. The book 4 .... stories about the people he meets with a 5 .... on how he feels from day to day. This is important, because he made the trip at a time in his life when he had a lot of personal problems. He wanted to 6 .... to himself that he could get on with life, even when things were going badly. At first, he found the trip difficult because he missed his family and friends. However, on each of the islands he visited, he stayed with a local 7 .... , and the people he met made him realise that life could be good, even under difficult circumstances. He 8 .... returned home a happier person.

Writing

Task 2

1 Look at this Writing task, then answer the questions which follow it.

In the past, people usually stayed in one place throughout their life. These days, people often move around. They often live in several different places in their lifetime. What are the advantages and disadvantages of both?

Give reasons for your answer and include any relevant information from your own knowledge and experience.

Write at least 250 words.

What should you do in this essay? Choose YES or NO.

1 Write about the past.	(YES)	NO
2 Write about the present.	YES	NO
3 Explain why people stayed in one place.	YES	NO
4 Describe the sort of places where people lived.	YES	NO
5 Explain why people move around more these days.	YES	NO
6 Say what is good and bad about both situations.	YES	NO
7 Give your own opinion.	YES	NO
8 Say why you have this opinion.	YES	NO
9 Give the opinion of other people.	YES	NO
10 Talk about your personal experiences.	YES	NO
11 Write a maximum of 250 words.	YES	NO

Unit 2

▶ Student's Book page 121

2 Look at this sample answer, and complete the gaps with words from the box. You will need to use some words more than once, and in some cases more than one answer is possible.

also	and	believe	but	however
opinion	think	view		

In the past, it was common for people to be born, grow up, live and die in the same place. This is still the case in some cultures, **1** *but* not in all.

I **2** *believe / think* that living in one place had its advantages. People were always close to their family and their friends. In small communities, people knew everyone well **3** .... they helped each other more. There was a real community spirit.

4 .... , there were disadvantages as well. For example, people probably got bored easily **5** .... there would not have been many job opportunities. **6** .... , when you had an argument with someone, you still had to see them every day. It would be difficult to get away from them.

Now, people are more mobile. In my country, people move from place to place much more. I **7** .... that this is a good thing, because they can learn more about the world and enjoy experiences that they would not have if they stayed in one place. They can **8** .... meet more people **9** .... they have better job opportunities. In my **10** .... , the main disadvantages are that people can lose touch with their family **11** .... it can be difficult to make new friends.

In my **12** .... , there are clear advantages and disadvantages to the way people lived in the past **13** .... the way they live now. I would not like to live in the same place all my life. **14** .... , I know some people who have done this **15** .... they are perfectly happy.

3 Look at the sample answer again. Has the candidate answered the question? Tick (✓) the boxes which are relevant.

The candidate

1 gives an introduction. ☐
2 writes about the past. ☐
3 writes about the present. ☐
4 says what is good and bad about both situations. ☐
5 gives their own opinion. ☐
6 talks about their personal experiences. ☐
7 gives a conclusion. ☐
8 has given a well-organised answer. ☐
9 has written at least 250 words. ☐

Spelling
Changes when adding *-ed*

1 How do you spell the past simple forms of these regular verbs? Complete the table with the verbs from the box.

admit	appear	carry	combine	end
memorise	miss	~~move~~	plan	play
prefer	prove	save	stop	study

Rule	Example	Past simple
1 Add *-d*	*move*	*moved*
2 Add *-ed*		
3 Change the last letter to *i* and add *-ed*		
4 Double the final letter and add *-ed*		

2 The words in brackets in these sentences each follow one of the rules in the table above. Write the words in their past simple forms.

1 I .... (try) Japanese food for the first time last night.
2 When she was eight, she .... (decide) she wanted to become a doctor.
3 When I was growing up, I (live) .... with my grandparents.
4 We .... (visit) all the sights during our trip to New York.
5 They met in 2003 and .... (marry) two years later.
6 As soon as she .... (arrive), everyone left.
7 Our friends only had a small house, so we .... (stay) in a hotel.
8 His strange behaviour really .... (worry) everyone.

Unit 3 Getting from A to B

Reading 1
Labelling a diagram

1 **You are going to read a passage about an airliner. Answer the question below.**

Read the title and subtitle and look at the picture. What do you think the passage will be about?
a an airliner that is not the same as other airliners
b reasons why a new airliner has been so successful
c the problems that a new type of airliner has been having

2 **Read the passage carefully. Complete labels (1–7) on the diagram. Choose NO MORE THAN TWO WORDS AND/OR A NUMBER from the passage for each answer.**

The Boeing 787

The Boeing 787 'Dreamliner' has been described as the airliner of the future. We look at the technology that makes it different

Until now, airliner fuselages have been made of aluminium sheets. Large aircraft can have 1,500 of these sheets with between 40,000 and 50,000 metal fasteners. The 787 is the first airliner to be built with a one-piece fuselage made from a special material called 'composite'. Not only does this make the airliner quicker and easier to build, but it also makes it a lot lighter. The advantage of this weight reduction is that the 787 uses 20 percent less fuel than other airliners of a similar size, which makes it much more environmentally friendly. The reduced weight also means that the Boeing 787 can fly further than many other airliners of a similar size, carrying 210 passengers or more up to 15,200 kilometres before refuelling.

Sometimes an airliner needs to change from one type of engine to another. This is a difficult and time-consuming process. The 787 has a revolutionary engine attachment on the wing which means that the engines can be changed in a much shorter time. The case containing the engine is also different from those on other airliners. It has been designed to cut down the noise from the engine, making it less noisy for passengers in the cabin as well as for people on the ground.

In addition to a quieter cabin, passengers will also benefit from windows which are 65 percent larger than those on other airliners, giving them a much better view of the world passing by below them. The windows also have a unique facility which allows passengers or cabin crew to control the amount of light that enters them. This is thanks to a liquid in the window which reacts to an electric current. When a passenger or cabin crew member presses a button, the current causes a chemical reaction in the window which darkens the liquid.

1 Composite fuselage material is much .... than traditional aluminium sheets.

2 Composite fuselage material reduces the amount of .... that the airliner needs.

3 Airliner can accommodate at least ....

4 Engineers can fit a new engine in a .... than it takes on other airliners.

5 A special engine case reduces ....

6 The size of the windows has increased by ....

7 Window glass can be made darker by passing an .... through them.

Reading 2
Matching headings

3 You are going to read a passage about city streets. Before you begin, look at the two pictures and answer the question.

What do you think the passage will be about?
a the difference between towns and cities now, and towns and cities in the past
b how towns and cities are planned and built
c removing cars and other vehicles from streets in towns and cities

4 Read the passage quickly and underline words 1–8. Then match them with their definitions, a–h.

1 pedestrians
2 exhaust fumes
3 experimenting
4 resistance
5 shopkeepers
6 construction
7 maintenance
8 outskirts

a trying something in order to discover what it is like
b the work that is done to keep something in good condition
c people who own or manage shops
d when people disagree with a change, idea, etc., and refuse to accept it
e the outer area of a city, town or village
f the work of building houses, offices, bridges, etc.
g people who are walking and not in a vehicle
h strong, unpleasant and often dangerous gases from vehicles

Pedestrians only
How traffic-free shopping streets developed

A The concept of traffic-free shopping areas goes back a long time. During the Middle Ages, traffic-free shopping areas known as souks were built in Middle Eastern countries to allow people to shop in comfort and, more importantly, safety. As far back as 2,000 years ago, road traffic was banned from central Rome during the day to allow for the free movement of pedestrians, and was only allowed in at night when shops and markets had closed for the day. In most other cities, however, pedestrians were forced to share the streets with horses, coaches and, later, with cars and other motorised vehicles.

B The modern, traffic-free shopping street was born in Europe in the 1960s, when both city populations and car ownership increased rapidly. Dirty exhaust fumes from cars and the risks involved in crossing the road were beginning to make shopping an unpleasant and dangerous experience. Many believed the time was right for experimenting with car-free streets, and shopping areas seemed the best place to start.

C At first, there was resistance from shopkeepers. They believed that such a move would be bad for business. They argued that people would avoid streets if they were unable to get to them in their cars. When the first streets in Europe were closed to traffic, there were even noisy demonstrations, as many shopkeepers predicted they would lose customers.

D However, research carried out afterwards in several European cities revealed some unexpected statistics. In Munich, Cologne and Hamburg, visitors to shopping areas increased by 50 percent. On Copenhagen's main shopping street, shopkeepers reported sales increases of 25–40 percent. Shopkeepers in Minneapolis, USA, were so impressed when they learnt this that they even offered to pay for the construction and maintenance costs of their own traffic-free streets.

E With the arrival of the traffic-free shopping street, many shops, especially those selling things like clothes, food and smaller luxury items, prospered. Unfortunately, it wasn't good news for everyone, as shops selling furniture and larger electrical appliances actually saw their sales drop. Many of these were forced to move elsewhere, away from the city centre. Today they are a common feature on the outskirts of towns and cities, often situated in out-of-town retail zones with their own car parks and other local facilities.

5 Now match the headings i–vii below with paragraphs A–E in the passage on page 19. There are two headings that you do not need.

	List of Headings
i	Facing local opposition
ii	Some reasons for success
iii	Winners and losers
iv	A need for change
v	An experiment that went wrong
vi	An idea from ancient history
vii	North America learns from Europe

Listening

Labelling a diagram

1 You are going to hear an information announcement for passengers on a train. Before you listen, look at the diagram below and answer these questions.

1 Where are you on the train? ....
2 Where is the engine? ....
3 What do we call the separate parts of the train where the passengers sit? Are they **A** cars, **B** carriages, **C** either of these?
4 What do we call a room on a train or a ship where you sleep? Is it **A** a cell, **B** a cabin, **C** an office?

2 (08) Now listen and label the diagram. Write ONE WORD ONLY for each answer.

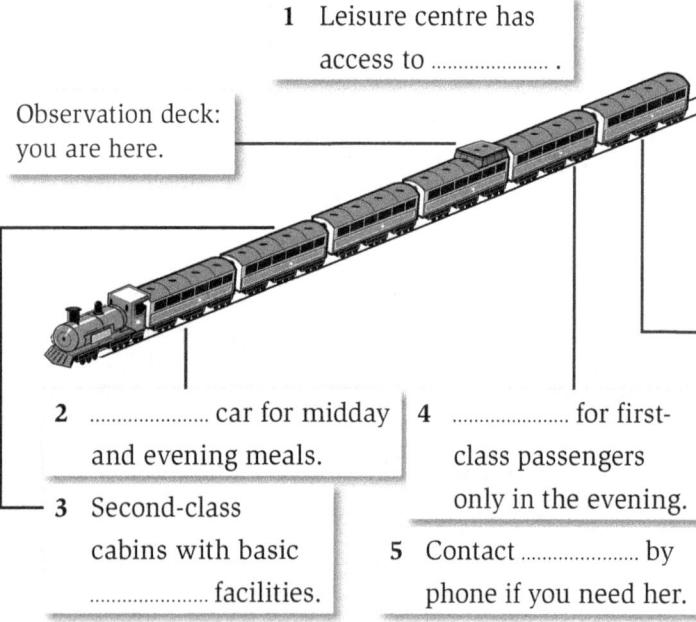

1 Leisure centre has access to ....
Observation deck: you are here.
2 .... car for midday and evening meals.
3 Second-class cabins with basic .... facilities.
4 .... for first-class passengers only in the evening.
5 Contact .... by phone if you need her.

Multiple choice

3 You are going to hear the next part of the information announcement. Before you listen, read Questions 1–5 and underline the key words in each question.

4 (09) Now listen and answer Questions 1–5. Choose the correct letter, A, B or C.

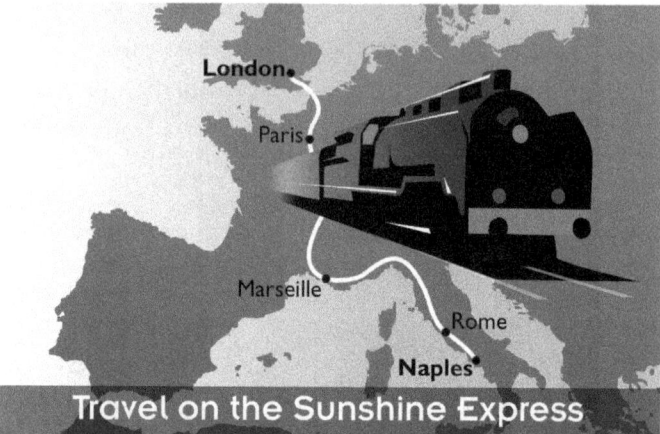

Travel on the Sunshine Express to Naples. Five-star luxury all the way!

1 How long will it take to get to Paris?
A about one hour
B about three hours
C about four hours

2 What should passengers do with their passports?
A leave them with their steward
B lock them away
C carry them at all times

3 When should passengers be in the restaurant car for dinner?
A 7.45 p.m.
B 8.00 p.m.
C 8.15 p.m.

4 What will the passengers do when the train gets to the Italian border?
A change trains
B go on a tour
C have lunch in a local café

5 What should passengers *not* do?
A eat their own food on the train
B open their cabin window
C leave the train before it gets to Italy

Unit 3

Vocabulary

make and *cause*

1 Complete this newspaper article with the correct form of *make* or *cause*.

Chaos on streets as traffic computer crashes ... again

A power cut **1** ...*caused*... the city's traffic control computer system to stop working again yesterday morning. This **2** .... enormous traffic jams throughout the city centre, as traffic lights stopped working. As well as **3** .... thousands of people late for work, the chaos on the streets also **4** .... a lot of accidents. Emergency vehicles were unable to reach accidents in time, since the traffic jams **5** .... it impossible for them to cross the city quickly. A driver we interviewed said, "The new computer system was supposed to **6** .... things easier for us, but since they started using it, it's just **7** .... so many problems. It never works properly. This kind of thing **8** .... me so angry."

Key vocabulary

2 Complete the passage using the words from the box.

| aim | alternative | competition | convenience |
| destination | pedestrians | ~~revolutionary~~ | unwilling |

London Underground's escalators

When London Underground railway's escalators were first installed in 1911, they were completely **1** ...*revolutionary*... . People had never seen anything like them before. Young people thought they were great fun, but many older passengers were **2** .... to use them because they thought they were dangerous. They were frightened the escalators would stop suddenly, and throw them all the way to the bottom. As a result, wherever possible, they used **3** .... forms of transport such as the bus or taxis.

Worried about losing their passengers to the **4** .... , London Underground managers employed a man with an artificial leg to ride up and down on the escalators all day. Their **5** .... was to prove that the escalators were safe. It worked, and the escalators became such a success that **6** .... started coming into stations from the street just to ride them. Today, the escalators are more than just a **7** .... More than three million people rely on London Underground trains to get them to and from their **8** .... every day, and the system would collapse without a fast and efficient way of getting them to and from the platforms.

Getting from A to B 21

Writing

Task 1

1 Look at this Writing task, and answer the questions which follow it.

The table and bar chart show how journey times in a city centre changed after improvements were made to the transport network, and the costs of using different forms of transport in the city.

Summarise the information by selecting and reporting the main features, and make comparisons where relevant.

Form of transport	Average journey time before improvements	Average journey time after improvements
Tram	22 minutes	16 minutes
Bus	28 minutes	23 minutes
Taxi	9 minutes	12 minutes
Car	10 minutes	15 minutes

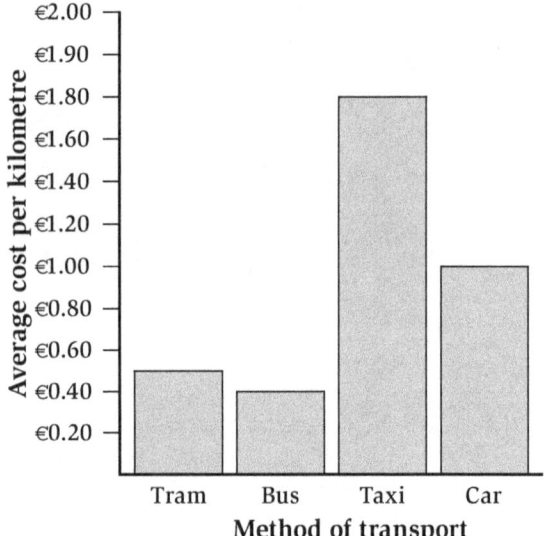

1 How many forms of transport are included in the table and bar chart?
   4 (tram, bus, taxi and car)

2 What was the fastest way of getting around the city *before* improvements to the transport network? ....

3 What was the fastest way of getting around the city *after* improvements to the transport network? ....

4 Do tram journeys take more time or less time than bus journeys? ....

5 How much on average does it cost to travel 1km by taxi? ....

6 Is it cheaper to travel by bus or by tram?
....

7 Which form of transport experienced the biggest rise in journey times after improvements to the network? ....

8 Which form of transport experienced the biggest fall in journey times after improvements to the network? ....

2 Refer to the table and bar chart on the left. Complete the sentences with words from the box. You will need to use some words more than once.

big   cheap   economical   expensive   fast   slow

1 Cost per kilometre: €0.40.
  The cheapest form of transport is the bus.

2 Average journey time: (before) 28 minutes; (after) 23 minutes.
  The bus is .... form of transport.

3 Cost per kilometre: €0.50.
  The tram is .... than the bus.

4 Average journey time: (before) 22 minutes; (after) 16 minutes.
  The tram is .... than the bus.

5 Cost per kilometre: €1.80.
  .... way of getting around the city is by taxi.

6 Average journey time: (before) 9 minutes; (after) 12 minutes.
  Taxis are .... way of getting around the city.

7 Average journey time: (before) 10 minutes; (after) 15 minutes.
  Cars have seen .... increase in journey times.

8 Average journey times: (before) 28 / 22 minutes; (after) 23 / 16 minutes.
  Journeys by bus and tram are .... than by car or taxi.

▶ Student's Book Unit 3 page 36

Unit 3

3 Complete the introduction from a sample answer to the Writing task with words and phrases from the box. You should use one word twice.

| bar graph | how long | how much | table |
| transport | travel | use | |

The **1** .... shows **2** .... it took to **3** .... around a city before and after the **4** .... network was improved. The **5** .... shows **6** .... it costs to **7** .... different forms of **8** .... in the city.

4 Now do the Writing task. Start your answer with the introduction in Exercise 3. Remember to:
- divide your answer into paragraphs
- include a brief conclusion.

Grammar
Making comparisons with adjectives and adverbs

1 Complete the second sentence in each pair so that it has a similar meaning to the first sentence, using a comparative adverb form of the words in bold.

1 It's **quicker** to get to London by train than by bus.
   You can get to London ...*more quickly*... by train than by bus.

2 Price rises are **steadier** this year than last year.
   Prices are rising .... this year than last year.

3 Grilling food is **healthier** than frying it.
   You'll eat .... if you grill food instead of frying it.

4 It is **easier** to travel into town by bus than by car.
   You can travel into town .... by bus than by car.

5 It's **more economical** to shop in the market than in the supermarket.
   You can shop .... in the market than in the supermarket.

2 Complete the passage with the correct comparative or superlative form of the words in brackets.

What do I think is **1** ...*the best*... (good) mode of transport? I think that depends on where and why I'm travelling. Obviously over long distances, I can get to my destination much **2** .... (quick) if I fly. Going the same distance by train is **3** .... (slow) than going by plane, but in my opinion this can be **4** .... (good), as I can get to see more of the country. Also, travelling by train is **5** .... (comfortable) form of transport because there's more room to move about. Without doubt, **6** .... (bad) method of transport, especially over long distances, has to be by bus. It's **7** .... (cheap) than going by train, but that's the only advantage I can think of. Of course, **8** .... (healthy) mode of transport is the bicycle. It may not be **9** .... (quick) way of getting around, and on some roads it's probably **10** .... (dangerous) way of travelling, but over short distances I don't think there's anything **11** .... (good). However, a bicycle is not very practical if you have to travel **12** .... (far) than a few kilometres.

Spelling
Changes when adding *-er* and *-est* to adjectives

Read the rules below. Number each adjective according to rules 1–5.

dangerous	4	enjoyable		expensive	
far		fast		good		healthy	
high		hot		lazy		sad	
slow		steady		thin			

1 Add *-er* or *-est*	cheap – cheaper – the cheapest
2 Change the last letter to *i*; add *-r* or *-est*	easy – easier – the easiest
3 Double the final letter; add *-er* or *-est*	big – bigger – the biggest
4 Add *more* or *the most*	comfortable – more comfortavble – the most comfortable
5 Change the word	bad – worse – the worst

Unit 4 It was all new once

Vocabulary

What type of word is it? 1

❶ Underline these words in the passage. Then decide what type of word each one is.

Word	Noun, verb or adjective?	Word	Noun, verb or adjective?
1 classic	adjective	6 rejected	
2 instructional		7 complex	
3 activist		8 persisted	
4 purpose		9 handmade	
5 accumulate		10 immense	

The story of Monopoly

Monopoly is one of the biggest-selling games in the world. It is sold in 80 countries and comes in 26 different languages. But where did this <u>classic</u> board game come from, and why did it become so popular?

At the beginning of the 20th century, an instructional game called 'The Landlord's Game' was first published by a political activist, Elizabeth Magie. The purpose of the game was to teach people how rich, powerful individuals take advantage of the poor while they accumulate even more wealth. Unfortunately, the game was not popular, and she sold very few copies of it.

In 1934, a man called Charles Darrow redesigned it, creating a game of chance. However, when he presented his game, which he called 'Monopoly', to the games manufacturers Parker Brothers, they rejected it. They said it was too complex and contained too many flaws.

Darrow persisted and decided to produce the game himself. He created and sold over 5,000 handmade sets to a local department store. The game had immense public appeal, and was so popular that Darrow went back to Parker Brothers, who bought the rights to the game.

❷ Which of the words from the passage are being defined here?

1 made by hand instead of by machine ...handmade...
2 something that teaches you about something ....
3 why you do something, or why something exists ....
4 refused to accept or agree with something ....
5 complicated and difficult to understand ....
6 extremely big, or a lot of something ....
7 someone who tries to cause social or political change ....
8 to increase in amount over a period of time ....
9 continued trying to do something in a determined way ....
10 popular for a long time and of high quality. ....

Key vocabulary

❸ Complete the sentences with the words and phrases from the box.

| cool | imitation | cite |
| take up | widespread | worldwide |

1 This isn't a real Rolex watch, just a cheap ...imitation... .
2 During my presentation, I'm going to .... the case of the people who invented the microchip.
3 The advantage of a small computer is that it doesn't .... too much space.
4 The popular project received .... support from the local community.
5 Tiny air holes in the wall let in breezes which .... the building on hot days.
6 .... sales of the game are twenty million every year.

Reading 1
Multiple choice

1 Read the passage about an invention quickly. Match the names of the people (1–5) with what they did (a–e).

1 John Loud
2 Ladislas Biro
3 Augustine Justo
4 Milton Reynolds
5 Patrick Frawley

a sold the first ballpoint pens in North America.
b wanted to make his job easier.
c achieved international success with his pen.
d invented the first pen with a rolling ball.
e asked someone to start a business in his country.

2 Read Questions 1–5. Do not read the options yet. Then find where each question is answered in the passage.

The ballpoint pen

Most of us have at least one, but how did this popular item evolve?

One morning in 1945, a crowd of 5,000 people jammed the entrance of Gimbels Department Store in New York. The day before, Gimbels had placed a full-page advertisement in the *New York Times* for a wonderful new invention, the ballpoint pen. The advertisement described the pen as 'fantastic' and 'miraculous'. Although they were expensive, $12.50 each, all 10,000 pens in stock were sold on the first day.

In fact, this 'new' pen was not new at all. In 1888, John Loud, a leather manufacturer, had invented a pen with a reservoir of ink and a rolling ball. However, his pen was never produced, and efforts by other people to produce a commercially successful one failed too. The main problem was with the ink. If it was too thin, the ink leaked out of the pen. If it was too thick, it didn't come out of the pen at all.

Almost fifty years later, in 1935, a newspaper editor in Hungary thought he spent too much time filling his pens with ink. He decided to invent a better kind of pen. With the help of his brother, who was a chemist, he produced a ballpoint pen that didn't leak when the pen wasn't being used. The editor was called Ladislas Biro, and it was his name that people would associate more than any other with the ballpoint pen.

By chance, Biro met Augustine Justo, the Argentinian president. Justo was so impressed with Biro's invention that he invited him to set up a factory in Argentina. In 1943, the first Biro pens were produced. Unfortunately, they were not popular, since the pen needed to be held in a vertical position for the ink to come out. Biro redesigned the pen with a better ball, and in 1944 the new product was on sale throughout Argentina.

It was a North American, Milton Reynolds, who introduced the ballpoint pen to the USA. Copying Biro's design, he produced the version that sold so well at Gimbels. Another American, Patrick Frawley, improved the design and in 1950 began producing a pen he called the *Papermate*. It was an immediate success, and within a few years, *Papermates* were selling in their millions around the world.

3 Now read each part carefully and choose the correct option, A, B, C or D.

1 People went to Gimbels to buy a ballpoint pen because
A they couldn't get them anywhere else.
B they had been told how good the pens were.
C they had never seen a ballpoint pen before.
D they thought the price was good.

2 Why were early ballpoint pens not produced commercially?
A Nobody wanted to buy one.
B It cost too much to produce them.
C They used too much ink.
D They didn't work properly.

3 Why was Ladislas Biro's pen better than earlier models?
A It didn't need to be filled with ink as often.
B It was designed by a chemist.
C The ink stayed in the pen until it was needed.
D It was easier to use.

4 Biro's first commercially-produced pen
A was produced in a factory owned by the Argentinian president.
B only worked if used in a certain way.
C was a major success.
D went on sale in 1944.

5 Patrick Frawley's pen
A was a better version of an earlier model.
B took time to become successful.
C was the USA's first commercially successful ballpoint pen.
D was only successful in the USA.

Reading 2
Summary completion

4 Quickly read the passage below, which is about a man called Marcel Bich.

1 What did Marcel Bich do?
....

2 How successful was he?
....

MARCEL BICH

The man who turned a luxury item into an everyday object

Marcel Bich, a French manufacturer of traditional ink pens, was the man who turned the ballpoint pen into an item that today almost anyone can afford. Bich was appalled at the poor quality of the ballpoint pens that were available, and was also shocked at their high cost. However, he recognised that the ballpoint was a firmly established invention, and he decided to design a cheap pen that worked well and would be commercially successful.

Bich went to the Biro brothers and asked them if he could use the design of their original invention in one of his own pens. In return, he offered to pay them every time he sold a pen. Then, for two years, Bich studied the detailed construction of every ballpoint pen that was being sold, often working with a microscope.

By 1950, he was ready to introduce his new wonder: a plastic pen with a clear barrel that wrote smoothly, did not leak and only cost a few cents. He called it the 'Bic Cristal'. The ballpoint pen had finally become a practical writing instrument. The public liked it immediately, and today it is as common as the pencil. In Britain, they are still called Biros, and many Bic models also say 'Biro' on the side of the pen, to remind people of their original inventors.

Bich became extremely wealthy thanks to his invention, which had worldwide appeal. Over the next 60 years his company, Société Bic, opened factories all over the world and expanded its range of inexpensive products. Today, Bic is as famous for its lighters and razors as it is for its pens, and you can even buy a Bic mobile phone.

5 Look at the summary of the passage in Exercise 6.

1 What type of word do you need in each gap?
2 Find the underlined words and numbers in the passage about Bich.

6 Now complete the summary. Choose NO MORE THAN TWO WORDS from the passage for each answer.

It is thanks to Marcel Bich that most people today are able to **1** .... a ballpoint pen. It was the bad quality and **2** .... of the pens which were available at the time that inspired him to design a **3** .... ballpoint pen that would be both inexpensive and reliable. After getting permission from the Biro brothers to base his pen on their **4** ...., he carefully **5** .... other ballpoints that were sold in the shops, and in 1950 introduced his own version, the 'Bic Cristal'. It was popular with the **6** ...., and Bich became very rich. His company, Bic, now makes a variety of cheap **7** ...., such as lighters and razors.

Listening
Sentence completion

1 Look at the sentences in Exercise 2 and decide what type of word (noun, verb or adjective) is missing from each sentence.

1 .... 2 .... 3 ....
4 .... 5 .... 6 ....

2 🔊 Listen and complete Questions 1–6. Write ONE WORD for each answer.

1 Joe's low .... doesn't allow him to buy many electronic goods.

2 He's often influenced by his .... when he buys electronic items.

3 Advertisements featuring somebody .... sometimes help him decide which product to buy.

4 Joe prefers to get new products from ....

5 He doesn't like waiting for a long time after .... something.

6 He finds it hard to resist buying electronic products if they are new and ....

Unit 4

Pick from a list

❸ Look at Questions 1–4 below. <u>Underline</u> the key words in each question.

Questions 1–4

1 What TWO things did Joe like about the mobile phone?
- A its colour
- B its size
- C its shape
- D its screen
- E its unique features

2 What TWO things does Joe usually look for when he buys a mobile phone?
- A It should be easy to use.
- B It should look good.
- C It should be cheap.
- D It should be reliable.
- E It should have a variety of games and other features.

3 Which TWO problems did Joe have with the radio?
- A It didn't sound good.
- B It wasn't loud enough.
- C It didn't pick up many radio stations.
- D He couldn't find anywhere to put it.
- E The control features didn't work properly.

4 What TWO things does Joe think would improve the computer?
- A making it smaller
- B reducing the price
- C increasing the memory
- D increasing the size of the keyboard
- E adding more features

❹ 🎧 Now listen to the next part of the interview with Joe. Choose TWO letters, A–E, for each question (1–4) in Exercise 3.

Grammar

Present perfect

❶ Complete these sentences with the correct form of the words in brackets. Use the past simple or present perfect.

1 Petrol prices ...*increased*... (increase) by 20% last year, and so far this year they've ......*gone*...... (go) up by another 30%.

2 I .... (have) a really awful meal last night, and I .... (feel) ill since I got up this morning.

3 Since websites like Facebook and Twitter .... (become) popular a few years ago, they .... (change) the way people communicate.

4 I .... (have) this camera for three months, and I still .... (not / learn) how to use it properly.

5 Where's Susan? I .... (not / see) her all day. .... (she / phone)?

6 Amy .... (not / come) to work yesterday, and she .... (not / be) at home when I .... (try) calling her last night.

7 I think people .... (become) too dependent on modern technology, and .... (forget) how to do many simple tasks.

8 .... (you / see) Tom this morning? He .... (borrow) my laptop a couple of days ago and I need it back.

❷ Complete these sentences with *for* or *since*.

1 I've lived here ......*since*...... I was born.
2 I've worked for the same company .... ages.
3 We haven't seen each other .... my birthday.
4 It hasn't stopped raining .... I got up today.
5 I've needed a new computer .... months.
6 Judy has lived abroad .... more than five years.
7 I've been on a diet .... April.
8 He moved to London in 2003, and he's lived there ever ....

3 Complete the gaps in this passage with the past simple or present perfect forms of the verbs in brackets. If there is no verb, use *for* or *since*.

Brian is my best friend. I **1** 've known (know) him **2** for years. We **3** .... (meet) at school, and we **4** .... (be) best friends ever **5** .... We **6** .... (do) so many great things together. In 2005 we **7** .... (travel) around the world together, and a couple of years later we **8** .... (run) the London Marathon together. We **9** .... (always / be) interested in computers, and nine months ago we **10** .... (set) up our own computer company. **11** .... then, we **12** .... (become) well-known among the big companies in our area, who **13** .... (use) our services several times. **14** .... the last two months, we **15** .... (have) a contract with IGH Bank. We're now so busy that we **16** .... (decide) to employ some extra staff.

Writing

Task 2

1 Here are some inventions which have changed or improved our lives. Match (1–11) with (A–K).

1 aspirin ☐   2 digital camera ☐   3 elastic band ☐
4 mobile phone ☐   5 paper ☐   6 paper clip ☐
7 pencil ☐   8 sticky tape ☐   9 syringe ☐
10 watch ☐   11 wheel ☐

2 Read this Writing task and <u>underline</u> the key ideas.

Most successful inventions do not rely on complicated technology. In fact, some of the world's greatest inventions have been very simple things.
To what extent do you agree or disagree?
Give reasons for your answer and include any relevant examples from your own knowledge or experience.

3 Number paragraphs A–E in the correct order to produce a sample answer to the Writing task.

A   Many other great inventions are even simpler. A wheel requires parts which move. This means that compared with a paper clip, an elastic band or a sheet of paper, it is quite complicated. But these smaller items are an essential part of every office. The same can be said for pencils, sticky tape, and many other stationery items.

This is paragraph ....

B   In conclusion, I believe that a great invention does not need to be complicated or technical. It can be something small or simple which has changed or improved our lives in some way. After all, most of us have a mobile phone, but it could not cure us if we became ill.

This is paragraph ....

C   However, many of the inventions which have changed our lives have been very simple things. Without the wheel, for example, we would not have cars, motorbikes or bicycles. Aeroplanes would not exist, as they would not be able to take off or land without wheels. Furthermore, wheels, in one form or another, are an important part of many smaller machines, like watches and computers.

This is paragraph ....

D   When people think of inventions, they often think of things which are technically complicated, or which require electricity in order to work. This is especially true in the 21st century, with our obsession for mobile phones, portable computers, digital cameras and other electronic items.

This is paragraph ......1......

> **E** Great simple inventions can also be found outside the office, of course. In my opinion, some of the most important inventions are those which have a medical purpose. Aspirin and syringes, for example, have helped to relieve pain and prevent or cure disease.
>
> This is paragraph ....

4 In which paragraph does the author

1. focus on inventions which he/she personally feels are extremely important? ....
2. summarise his/her opinions and give reasons for those opinions? ....
3. discuss several very small, very simple inventions? ....
4. give an example of an invention that has been an important part of other inventions? ....
5. introduce the subject by giving a popular definition of an invention? ....

5 Now write your answer to this Writing task. You should write at least 250 words.

> Write about the following topic.
>
> *The Internet is probably the most significant invention of the last 30 years. Without it, our lives would be completely different.*
>
> *To what extent do you agree or disagree?*
>
> Give reasons for your answer and include any relevant examples from your own knowledge or experience.

Spelling
Using and misusing double letters

These sentences each contain a word that is spelt incorrectly. <u>Underline</u> the words, and write them correctly at the end of the sentences.

1. The two computers are so similar that it's difficult to tell them <u>appart</u>. .... *apart* ....
2. Email is a much quicker and more eficient way of contacting people than sending a letter. ....
3. If the company is sucessful, they plan to open offices around the world. ....
4. Nobody paid her invention much atention at the time, but gradually people realised how useful it would be. ....
5. Detailed research suggests that sitting in front of a computer all day can be harmfull to your health. ....
6. The company atempted to invent a suitable substitute for sugar, but the result tasted more like salt. ....
7. I find it so anoying when you're in the middle of writing an email and your computer suddenly stops working. ....
8. Air bags and seat belts in cars have saved thousands of people from death and serious injury in road acidents. ....
9. I had no physicall injuries after the car crash, but I was in a terrible state of shock for several days. ....
10. Ever since the new air conditioning was instaled, people in the office have been suffering from bad headaches. ....
11. Thanks to modern information technology, we can now comunicate instantly with people on the other side of the world. ....
12. There's a sign by the school entrance that says 'Wellcome to the West Lake English Centre'. ....
13. His atendance was always poor, and his attempts to blame it on other people made him very unpopular. ....

Unit 5 Animal world

Reading 1
Sentence completion

1 Quickly read the passage on the right and answer these questions.

1 Where do honey badgers live?
....
2 What do they look like?
....
3 Why is 'honey badger' not a good name for this animal?
....

2 Read Questions 1–8 below.

1 <u>Underline</u> the key words.
2 Decide what type of information you need for each gap.

Questions 1–8

1 Although they are not big animals, honey badgers are fearless, ... and tough.
2 Honey badgers will attack .... if they need to protect themselves.
3 The pattern and colours on the honey badger's back make it ....
4 The food they eat is meat-based and ....
5 .... form the biggest part of a honey badger's diet.
6 Honey badgers find the creatures they eat by their ....
7 .... are often used to catch honey badgers which attack beehives.
8 For one particular type of food, the honey badger has a .... with another creature.

The honey badger

It looks harmless and vulnerable. But the honey badger is afraid of nothing… and will attack and eat almost anything

The honey badger (*Melivora capensis*), is an African and south-Asian mammal that has a reputation for being one of the world's most fearless animals, despite its small size. And in spite of its gentle-sounding name, it is also one of its most aggressive. Honey badgers have been known to attack lions, buffalo, and snakes three times their size. Even humans are not safe from a honey badger if it thinks the human will attack or harm it. They are also extremely tough creatures, and can recover quickly from injuries that would kill most other animals.

At first glance, honey badgers look like the common European badger. They are usually between 75cm and 1 metre long, although males are about twice the size of females. They are instantly recognisable by grey and white stripes that extend from the top of the head to the tail. Closer inspection, which is probably not a wise thing to do, reveals pointed teeth, and sharp front claws which can be four centimetres in length.

Honey badgers are meat-eating animals with an extremely varied diet. They mainly eat a range of small creatures like beetles, lizards and birds, but will also catch larger reptiles like snakes and small crocodiles. Some mammals, such as foxes, antelope and wild cats also form part of their diet.

The badgers locate their prey mainly using their excellent sense of smell, and catch most of their prey through digging. During a 24-hour period, they may dig as many as fifty holes, and travel more than 40 kilometres. They are also good climbers, and can easily climb very tall trees to steal eggs from birds' nests, or catch other tree-dwelling creatures.

As their name suggests, honey badgers have always been associated with honey, although they do not actually eat it. It is the highly nutritious bee eggs (called 'brood') that they prefer, and they will do anything to find it. They usually cause a lot of damage to the hive in the process, and for this reason, humans are one of their main predators. Bee-keepers will often set special traps for honey badgers, to protect their hives.

One of the most fascinating aspects of the honey badger is its working relationship with a bird called the greater honeyguide (*Indicator indicator*). This bird deliberately guides the badger to beehives, then waits while the badger breaks into the hive and extracts the brood. The two creatures, bird and mammal, then share the brood between them.

❸ Now complete Questions 1–8. Write NO MORE THAN TWO WORDS from the passage for each answer.

Reading 2
Pick from a list

❹ You are going to read more about the honey badger. Before you do this, look at the exam question in the box and answer the questions 1-4.

> 1 Why did the wildlife experts visit the Kalahari desert? Choose two reasons.
> A To find where honey badgers live.
> B To observe how honey badgers behave.
> C To try to change the way honey badgers behave.
> D To temporarily catch some honey badgers.
> E To find out why honey badgers have such a bad reputation.

1 Underline the key words in the question.
2 Find the paragraph in the passage where the question is dealt with.
3 Now look at these five options for the question above. Look for the answers in the text. Delete three answers which are NOT possible.
4 Which two options are you left with?
   .... and ....

On the trail of the honey badger

Researchers learn more about this fearless African predator

On a recent field trip to the Kalahari Desert, a team of researchers learnt a lot more about honey badgers. They were rewarded with a detailed insight into how these fascinating creatures live and hunt.

The team employed a local wildlife expert, Kitso Khama, to help them locate and follow the badgers across the desert. Their main aim was to study the badgers' movements and behaviour as discreetly as possible, without frightening them away or causing them to change their natural behaviour. They also planned to trap a few and study them close up before releasing them. In view of the animal's reputation, this was something that even Khama was reluctant to do.

'The problem with honey badgers is they are naturally curious animals, especially when they see something new,' he says. 'That, combined with their unpredictable nature, can be a dangerous mixture. If they sense you have food, for example, they won't be shy about coming right up to you for something to eat. They're actually quite sociable creatures around humans, but as soon as they feel they might be in danger, they can become extremely vicious. Fortunately this is rare, but it does happen.'

The research confirmed many things that were already known. As expected, honey badgers ate any creatures they could catch and kill. Even poisonous snakes, feared and avoided by most other animals, were not safe from them. The researchers were surprised, however, by the animal's fondness for local melons, probably because of their high water content. Previously researchers thought that the animal got all of its liquid requirements from its prey. The team also learnt that, contrary to previous research findings, the badgers occasionally formed loose family groups. They were also able to confirm certain results from previous research, including the fact that female badgers never socialised with each other.

Following some of the male badgers was a challenge, since they can cover large distances in a short space of time. Some hunting territories cover more than 500 square kilometres. Although they seem happy to share these territories with other males, there are occasional fights over an important food source, and male badgers can be as aggressive towards each other as they are towards other species.

As the badgers became accustomed to the presence of people, it gave the team the chance to get up close to them without being the subject of the animals' curiosity – or their sudden aggression. The badgers' eating patterns, which had been disrupted, returned to normal. It also allowed the team to observe more closely some of the other creatures that form working associations with the honey badger, as these seemed to adopt the badgers' relaxed attitude when near humans.

❺ Read the rest of the passage and choose TWO letters, A–E, for Questions 2–5.

> Questions 2–5
> 2 What two things does Kitso Khama say about honey badgers?
> A They show interest in things they are not familiar with.
> B It's hard to tell how they will behave.
> C They are always looking for food.

Animal world

D They do not enjoy human company.
E It is common for them to attack people.

3 What two things did the team find out about honey badgers?
A There are some creatures they will not eat.
B They were afraid of poisonous creatures.
C They may get some of the water they need from fruit.
D They do not always live alone.
E Female badgers do not mix with male badgers.

4 According to the passage, which of these two features are typical of male badgers?
A They don't run very quickly.
B They hunt over a very large area.
C They defend their territory from other badgers.
D They sometimes fight each other.
E They are more aggressive than females.

5 What two things happened when the honey badgers got used to humans being around them?
A The badgers lost interest in people.
B The badgers became less aggressive towards other creatures.
C The badgers started eating more.
D Other animals started working with the badgers.
E Other animals near them became more relaxed.

Listening

Table completion

1 You are going to hear a college head teacher giving information to some students about a college event. Before you listen, look at the table. What kind of information do you need for each gap?

Natural History day: morning events
All events begin at 9.30. You **must** attend one of these.

Name of event	Theme or topic	Type of event	Location
Dogs might fly	Animal 1	Lecture and 2	Room 27
Flowers talk	How plants might 3	Video presentation	4 ....
A world in your 5	Local animal and plant life	6	Local park
I'm not touching that	Snakes and other 7	Workshop	8 .... lab

2 🔊 Now listen and complete the table above. Write NO MORE THAN TWO WORDS OR A NUMBER for each answer.

Labelling a plan

3 How do you get to room F from the main hall? Complete these directions with words from the box. There is one word you do not need, and there is one word you will need to use twice.

| end | first | follow | leave | left | opposite |
| pass | right | second | turn | | |

1 .... the main hall by the door 2 .... reception and 3 .... left. 4 .... the corridor until you 5 .... Room J, and turn 6 .... At the 7 .... of the corridor, turn 8 .... Room F is through the 9 .... door on your 10 ....

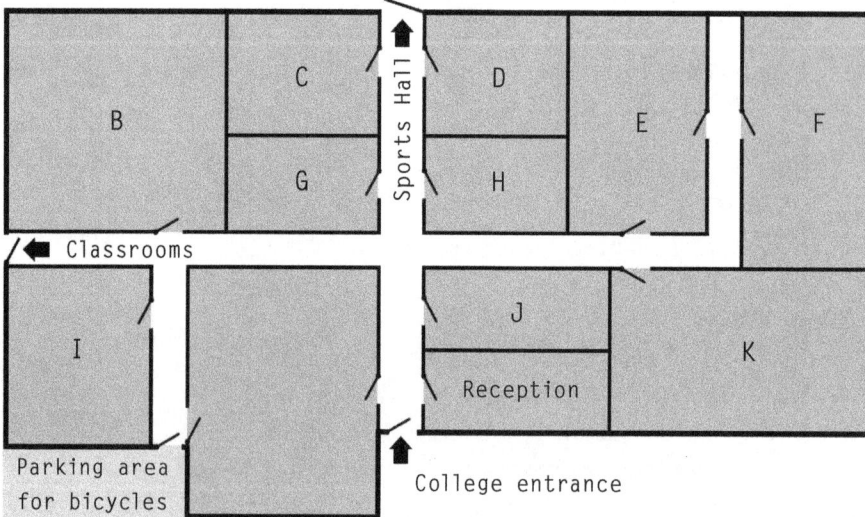

▶ Student's Book page 124

4 🎧 **Now listen and label the plan. Write the correct letter, A–K, next to Questions 1–5.**

1 Administration office ....
2 Café ....
3 Student common room ....
4 Lockers ....
5 Library ....

Vocabulary

What type of word is it? 2

1 **Look at the endings of the words in bold in each of these sentences. Decide if they are nouns, verbs, adjectives or adverbs.**

1 I'm sorry, but I **accidentally** broke your favourite cup. ....adverb....

2 Rats can be very **aggressive** creatures when they feel threatened. ....

3 Can I have your **attention**, everyone, please? ....

4 We decided to **celebrate** his birthday with a big party. ....

5 It's hard to work with that **continuous** noise in the background. ....

6 There's an excellent **cultural** centre in our city. ....

7 He's a keen **environmentalist**, and spends a lot of time working with animals. ....

8 A good **teacher** should listen as well as talk. ....

2 **Complete the table with *nouns, verbs, adjectives* or *adverbs*, using Exercise 1 as a guide.**

Words which end in		are often	
	1 -ate		....verbs....
	2 -ist		....
	3 -ion		....
	4 -er		....
	5 -ive		....
	6 -ly		....
	7 -ous		....
	8 -al		....

3 **Complete these sentences with the correct form of the words in brackets.**

1 I've never been very ....ambitious.... (ambition) and would be quite happy working in an office.

2 There are two main .... (politics) parties in my country.

3 I would love to be a wildlife .... (photograph).

4 You should ask your .... (pharmacy) if he can give you something for your cough.

5 When you give a talk, it's a good idea to .... (illustration) it with pictures.

6 After six hours on the road, we .... (final) arrived at the nature reserve.

7 She's very .... (talk) but never seems to listen.

8 He led an .... (adventure) life and wrote a lot of books.

9 After a brief .... (introduce), she began her talk.

10 I always feel really .... (nerves) before an exam.

Key vocabulary

4 **Replace the words and phrases in *italics* with words and phrases from the box which have a similar meaning.**

archives	brilliant	colony	came upon
estimate	get rid of	hostile	
harmless	indicates	risky	shift	~~spotted~~

1 On the journey we *saw* several leopards and a couple of lions. ....spotted....

2 We need to *move* these boxes into another room. ....

3 Working with poisonous snakes can be quite *dangerous*. ....

4 Recent evidence *shows* that elephant numbers on the reserve are rising. ....

5 Many people are afraid of spiders, even though most of them are *not dangerous*. ....

6 We *guess* that the land will take at least five years to recover from the fire. ....

Animal world 33

7 The research team *found* a species of bird that everyone thought was extinct. ....

8 Annual rainfall figures going back to 1887 can be found in the national *records*. ....

9 The frog we found was yellow, with *very bright* pink markings. ....

10 We need to *throw away* all of this rubbish as soon as possible. ....

11 The lizard is able to survive in very *unpleasant and dangerous* environments. ....

12 If you disturb a *group* of red ants, they are likely to attack you. ....

Writing

Task 1

1 Complete these sentences with *increased* or *fell*, and then underline the best preposition in bold to complete the sentences. In <u>one</u> sentence, <u>both</u> of the prepositions are correct.

1 The number of fish caught in the lake .... **from / in** 2010.

> 2009: 17,000 fish caught in the lake.
> 2010: 15,000 fish caught in the lake.

2 The amount of honey produced .... **from / in** July.

> June: Amount of honey produced – 170kg.
> July: amount of honey produced – 190kg.

3 The number of animals on the reserve .... **between / from** 2005 and 2007.

> 2005: 1250 animals on the game reserve
> 2006: 1520 animals on the game reserve
> 2007: 1870 animals on the game reserve

4 **Between / From** 2004 to 2006, the number of visitors to the zoo ....

5 **During / Over** the same period, admission prices ....

> 2004: 20,000 visitors to the zoo. Admission price: £10
> 2005: 18,000 visitors to the zoo. Admission price: £12
> 2006: 16,000 visitors to the zoo. Admission price: £15

▶ Student's Book page 126

2 Look at the Writing task below, and complete the sentences on page 35. Use the words and phrases in the box to form an opening paragraph. You will need to use one phrase twice.

> *The charts below show information about the number of fish caught and the number of fishing boats used in Westhaven.*
>
> *Summarise the information by selecting and reporting the main features and make comparisons where relevant.*

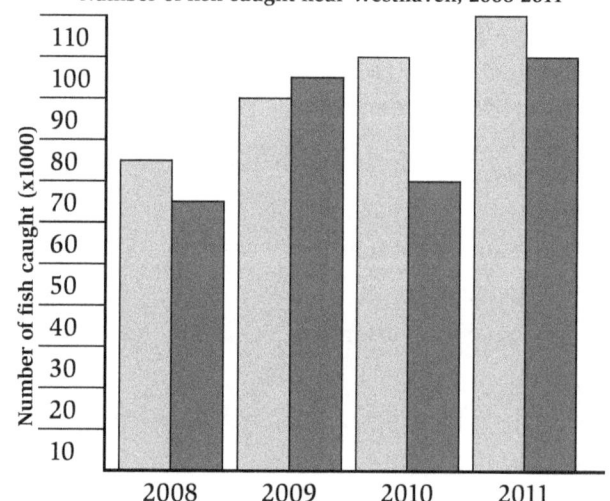

 = Tuna    = Swordfish

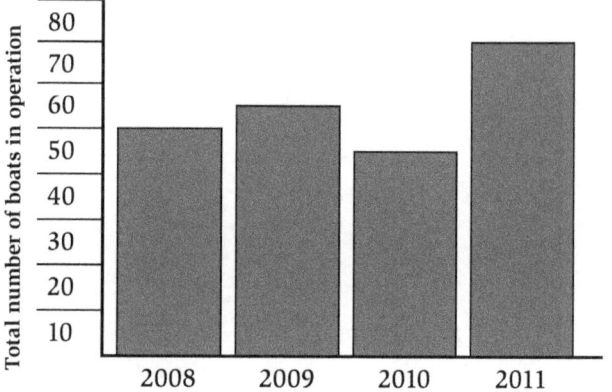

| and | between | during | first | fishing boats |
| how many | same | second | swordfish | tuna |

The 1 ..*first*.. chart shows 2 .... 3 .... and 4 .... were caught near Westhaven 5 .... 2008 6 .... 2011. The 7 .... chart shows 8 .... 9 .... there were in Westhaven 10 .... the 11 .... period.

3 Complete the sentences with words from the box to form a concluding paragraph. You will need to use some words more than once.

| however | more | number | overall |
| swordfish | tuna | | |

1 ..*Overall*.. , the 2 .... of fishing boats that were used did not affect the 3 .... of 4 .... which were caught. 5 .... , it did appear to affect the 6 .... of 7 .... When there were 8 .... boats, 9 .... 10 .... were caught.

4 Now write the main part of the answer in about 70 words. Remember to include information from both charts.

Grammar
Countable and uncountable nouns

1 Are these words used with *countable* or *uncountable* nouns? Underline the correct option.

1 amount: countable / <u>uncountable</u>
2 few: countable / uncountable
3 fewer: countable / uncountable
4 less: countable / uncountable
5 little: countable / uncountable
6 many: countable / uncountable
7 much: countable / uncountable
8 number: countable / uncountable

2 Complete these sentences with the words in Exercise 1.

1 There were ..*fewer*.. visitors to the zoo this year than there were last year.
2 A large .... of dolphins and whales are accidentally killed by fishermen each year.
3 There are a .... species of animal which are so fearless they will attack other animals which are much bigger than them.
4 How .... research did you do before you wrote your essay on birds of prey?
5 The project to study wildlife in the region will take a huge .... of time to complete.
6 There were so .... visitors to the wildlife reserve last year that a decision had to be made to restrict their numbers.
7 If you want to get fit, you should eat .... chocolate and get more exercise.
8 Unfortunately, we were given very .... information before our trip to the Kalahari.

Spelling
Small words often misspelled

This passage contains ten small spelling mistakes. Underline the words which are spelled incorrectly, and write the correct spellings above.

Last year I visited the Galapagos Islands on a college trip. We flew from London <u>too</u> Madrid, than
to
transferred onto a flight to Ecuador's capital, Quito. From their, it was another flight to Baltra, one of the biggest islands in they group. It was much more crowded their then I expected, with lots of tour groups everywhere. However, things changed when we left Baltra and went too the other islands. The were much less crowded. We were able to study lots of unusual animals in there natural environment. We met some scientists working on the islands to, and learnt a lot of interesting things from them.

Unit 6 Being human

Reading 1

Yes / No / Not Given

1 You are going to read a passage about bad habits. Read the title and subheading first. What do you think the writer is going to say about bad habits?

a Most people have bad habits that they'd like to break.

b It can be extremely hard to break a bad habit.

c People pick up most of their bad habits while they are growing up.

d People are not always aware that they have bad habits.

Breaking the habit

We all think we can break our bad habits – but they can stay with us for life

What is a bad habit? The most common definition is that it is something that we do regularly, almost without thinking about it, and which has some sort of negative consequence. This consequence could affect those around us, or it could affect us personally. Those who deny having bad habits are probably lying. Bad habits are part of what makes us human.

Many early habits, like sucking our thumb, are broken when we are very young. We are either told to stop doing it by our parents, or we consciously or subconsciously observe that others do not have the same habit, and we gradually grow out of it. It is when we intentionally or unintentionally pick up new habits in our later childhood or early adulthood that it becomes a problem. Unless we can break that habit early on, it becomes a part of our life, and becomes 'programmed' into our brain.

A recent study of human memory suggests that no matter how hard we try to change our habits, it is the old ways that tend to win, especially in situations where we are rushed, stressed or overworked. Habits that we thought we had got rid of can suddenly come back. During the study programme, the researchers showed a group of volunteers several pictures, and gave them words to associate with them (for example, see a picture of tea, and associate it with 'breakfast'). They then showed the volunteers the same pictures again, and gave them new words to associate with them (see a picture of tea, and say 'afternoon').

A few days later, the volunteers were given a test. The researchers showed them the pictures, and told them to respond with one of the words they had been given for each one. It came as no surprise that their answers were split between the first set of words and the second. Two weeks later, they were given the same test again. This time, most of them only gave the first set of words. They appeared to have completely forgotten the second set.

The study confirms that the responses we learn first are those that remain strongest over time. We may try to change our ways, but after a while, the response that comes to mind first is usually the first one we learned. The more that response is used, the more automatic it becomes and the harder it becomes to respond in any other way.

The study therefore suggests that over time, our bad habits also become automatic, learned behaviour. This is not good news for people who picked up bad habits early in life and now want to change or break them. Even when we try to put new, good intentions into practice, those previously learned habits remain stronger in more automatic, unconscious forms of memory.

❷ Read Questions 1–7 below and underline the words that you think will help you find the right place in the passage.

Questions 1–7

Do the following statements agree with the claims of the writer in the Reading passage?

Write

YES   if the statement agrees with the claims of the writer

NO   if the statement contradicts the claims of the writer

NOT GIVEN if it is impossible to say what the writer thinks about this

1 We usually develop bad habits when we are very young.
2 We can only break bad habits if people tell us to do so.
3 Bad habits may return when we are under pressure.
4 Researchers were surprised by the answers that the volunteers gave in the first test.
5 The volunteers found the test more difficult when they did it the second time.
6 People find it more difficult to remember things they learnt when they were young.
7 If we develop bad habits early in life, they are harder to get rid of.

❸ Now answer Questions 1–7.

Reading 2

Summary completion with a box

❹ Find the words in bold in the passage on the right and match them to the following definitions.

1 to do or make something which behaves or looks like something real, but which is not real
2 the work of treating mental or physical illness without surgery
3 using computer images and sounds that make you think an imagined situation or object is real
4 to make someone experience something or be affected by it
5 an extreme fear of something
6 someone whose job is to treat a particular type of mental or physical illness

Fighting fear using virtual reality

Computers are not just for entertainment, shopping or research purposes – as one woman found out when she tried to cure her fears

Most people have at least one thing they are afraid of. A fear of things like snakes, spiders, dogs, heights or open spaces affects over 90% of the population. In extreme cases, a fear can develop into a **phobia**, where the fear of something is so powerful it can affect the way the sufferer lives their life. About 10% of people suffer from a phobia. Most sufferers never seek treatment, because the most common type of cure – 'exposure therapy' – involves them being **exposed** to the object of their fear, and this is the last thing many of them are prepared to do.

There is now a new cure for phobias, using something called **virtual** reality exposure **therapy** (VRET). The concept is simple. The person with the phobia wears a virtual reality headset. A computer, controlled by a **therapist**, then **simulates** a variety of situations in which the sufferer is gradually exposed to the object of their fear, which they view on the headset's screen. At the same time, the therapist explains why they should not be afraid of it. The technique is surprisingly successful, as this case demonstrates.

Sara Considine had a serious spider phobia, and had developed several spider-related behaviour patterns. Before going to bed, for example, she would check her room for spiders, then seal the windows with tape so none could get in. She had frightening dreams about spiders every night. Eventually, she decided to get treatment.

During twelve one-hour virtual reality sessions over a three-month period, Ms Considine started very slowly. First, she stood a long way from the virtual spider and just looked at it. Slowly, she moved a little closer. The therapist controlling the computer programme then made the virtual spider move. After just two sessions, Ms Considine reported that although she still saw spiders in her dreams, they were no longer frightening, and she had even managed to have an amusing 'conversation' with one of them. A few sessions later, the therapist encouraged her to hold the virtual spider in her virtual hand, and put it in places where the presence of a real spider would cause her fear. The next stage was to introduce touch. A large toy spider was placed next to her. Ms Considine then reached out to touch the virtual spider she could see on the screen, and at the same time her real hand touched the toy spider.

After her sessions were over, Sara Considine was able to stop her spider-related behaviour. She even took up camping, something she would never have considered before therapy. More recently she has appeared on a television nature programme, where for the first time she was able to hold a real spider in her hands.

5 Now find the part of the passage that deals with Sara Considine's VRET treatment course and answer Questions 1–5.

Questions 1–5

Complete the summary using the list of words and phrases, A–J, below.

Treating a phobia using VRET

Sara Considine's programme of treatments lasted for **1** .... months. At first, the sessions did not move very **2** .... , as she just **3** .... the virtual spider through her headset. It only took two sessions for her to stop being **4** .... the spiders in her dreams. After a while, she could hold the virtual spider in her virtual hand, and the next stage involved making physical **5** .... with a toy spider.

A	afraid of	F	quickly
B	amused by	G	slowly
C	contact	H	touch
D	held	I	three
E	observed	J	twelve

Listening

Matching

1 You are going to hear a conversation between two friends, Matt and Amy. They are talking about the things that make people happy. Read Questions 1–4 in the Listening task. Then complete this description of what you will hear and what you must do.

I am going to hear two friends called Matt and Amy having a **1** .... In it, they will mention the names of four **2** .... , and the things that they believe make people feel **3** .... As I listen, I must choose **4** .... things from the box, and write the letters next to **5** .... 1–4. There are **6** .... things in the box that I do not need.

Questions 1–4

What do these experts say makes people happy?

Choose FOUR answers from the box and write the correct letter, A–F, next to Questions 1–4.

Experts

1. Richard Tunney ....
2. Martin Seligman ....
3. George Vaillant ....
4. Melanie Hodgson ....

What makes people happy

A having an achievable ambition
B being on holiday
C helping other people
D making new friends
E planning a trip
F having a social life

2 Now listen to the conversation and answer Questions 1–4.

Pick from a list

3 You are going to hear the next part of the conversation between Matt and Amy. Look at Questions 5–10 below and <u>underline</u> the key words in each question. Then quickly read through the options.

Questions 5–10

Choose TWO letters, A–E.

Questions 5–6

What does Amy think about personality tests? Choose TWO things.

A They take too much time to do.
B They are not accurate.
C They are entertaining.
D They are too serious.
E They tell you unexpected things.

Questions 7–8

What TWO things make Amy happy?

A being with friends
B having time on her own
C going out with her family
D spending time outside
E keeping fit

Unit 6

Questions 9–10

What **TWO** things is Matt going to do next?

A get more information
B go to the library
C try to find some useful books
D take a short break
E ask someone for help

❹ 🎧15 Now listen and answer Questions 5–10.

Vocabulary
Word building

❶ Each of these sentences contains a wrong word form. <u>Underline</u> the word in each sentence, then write its *correct* form in the crossword grid.

1 You feel a great sense of <u>achieve</u> when you pass an exam. *achievement*
2 She was a skill artist who could produce beautiful paintings.
3 Sara Considine successful overcame her fear of spiders.
4 People who regular take a holiday perform better at work.
5 People who spend their lives seeking famous and fortune are often very unhappy.
6 I'd rather be really talent at one thing than just good at many things.
7 Some people think that naturally programmes on television are boring, but I love them.
8 Hard work people are often happier than lazy ones.

Key vocabulary

❷ Complete this personal diary entry with the words and phrases from the box.

plans	daily routine	tried	familiar
fell asleep	get to the top	good at
key to success	unexpected

Dear Diary,

It's been another typical Monday. The same **1** .... I got up and went to work, where I had to deal with the same old problems and talk to the same old **2** .... faces. After work, I went for a walk in the park, and then came home again, where I was so tired I **3** .... as soon as I sat down. As usual, nothing **4** .... or exciting happened. My life is so boring. I don't have any hobbies and I rarely see my friends. Perhaps I should change. Everyone says that ambition is the **5** .... If I **6** .... harder at work, perhaps I could **7** .... Or perhaps I should make some **8** .... and look for another job. The problem is that I don't seem to be very **9** .... anything else. Oh well, it's time for bed now. Perhaps tomorrow will be a better day.

Writing
Task 2

❶ Read this Writing task. Put the sentences in the sample answer that follows it into their correct order.

Write about the following topic.

Some people believe that our happiness depends on how much money we have. Others say that 'money cannot buy happiness'.

Do you think that having money is the key to happiness, or are there more important factors?

Give reasons for your answer and include any relevant examples from your own knowledge or experience.

▶ Student's Book page 127

Being human 39

Sample answer

Introduction

a Everybody needs money. ....1........

b We also need it to pay for the luxuries that we all enjoy, such as a cinema visit or a meal in a restaurant. ....

c We spend eight hours a day or more earning it so that we can pay our bills and buy essentials. ....

First main paragraph

a Is money therefore the key to happiness? ....1........

b These include football players, actors and rock stars. ....

c However, this is not the same as being happy. ....

d In fact, if you believe the newspaper stories about them, many are often rude and aggressive. ....

e If they are happy, they do not seem to show it. ....

f There are many wealthy people in my country. ....

g It is certainly true that it can buy us comfort and security. ....

h This is not the sort of behaviour that we associate with happiness. ....8........

Second main paragraph

a Therefore, if happiness does not depend on money, what factors does it depend on? ....1........

b Some people are happy because they have good friends and enjoy an active social life. ....

c Having money, for me at least, does not make me any more or any less happy. ....

d Others find happiness by helping others, or by doing a job that they really enjoy. ....

e Speaking personally, I am happy when doing simple things like listening to music or going for a walk. ....5........

f This probably depends on the individual. ....

Conclusion

a In conclusion, I think that there may well be a few cases where someone's happiness depends on their wealth. ....1........

b As everyone is different, these probably vary from person to person. ....

c However, this is probably rare. ....

d For most people, other factors are far more important. ....

2 Now write your own answer to the following Writing task. Write at least 250 words.

> **Write about the following topic.**
>
> *Some people say that in order to be happy, you must have a job you love doing. Others say that other factors are more important.*
>
> *Do you think that people can only be happy if they have a job they really enjoy?*
>
> **Give reasons for your answer and include any relevant examples from your own knowledge or experience.**

Grammar

Zero and first conditionals (if / unless)

1 Complete these sentences with *if* or *unless*.

1 .... I get the chance later, I'll call you.

2 People never get very far in life .... they have motivation.

3 .... you know someone well, you shouldn't ask them personal questions.

4 I'll feel happier .... I know you have arrived safely.

5 Some people get embarrassed .... they don't understand something properly.

6 .... I have an urgent appointment or am late, I always walk instead of taking the car.

7 .... she has therapy, she'll always be afraid of spiders.

8 .... I have a child, I won't let it suck its thumb.

② Match the two halves of the conditional sentences in the box below. Then use the sentences to complete the dialogues, 1–8.

1st clause

a If you start eating less and get some exercise,
b People get bored
c Giving up something is almost impossible
d If you don't know what a word means,
e If you don't ask her,
f Unless he comes in the next five minutes,
g They can't do that
h If I don't get this work done,

2nd clause

i   you should first try to guess its meaning from its context.
ii   unless you make a real effort.
iii you'll never know.
iv   we'll have to go without him.
v   I'll be in trouble.
vi   if they see the same, old familiar faces every day.
vii unless they have a good reason.
viii you'll lose the weight you've put on.

1 **A:** We're all going out tonight. Do you want to join us?
   B: Thanks, but I can't. …h…+…v…

2 **A:** I was in town yesterday, when the police stopped me and asked for some identification. When I asked why, they wouldn't tell me.
   B: That's not right. ……… + ………

3 **A:** I weighed myself this morning. I've put on three kilos in the last month.
   B: Well, there's a simple solution.
   ……… + ………

4 **A:** I've got problems with reading. I spend a lot of time looking up words in the dictionary.
   B: That's not always the best way.
   ……… + ………

5 **A:** Where's Alan? He was supposed to be here ten minutes ago.
   I don't know. ……… + ………

6 **A:** I stopped eating red meat a couple of months ago, but last night I went out for dinner. Before I knew it, I was eating a large, juicy steak.
   B: You obviously don't have the willpower.
   ……… + ………

7 **A:** Sometimes I go into work, look at my colleagues and think to myself "Oh no, not again."
   B: That's normal. ……… + ………

8 **A:** I want to earn more money, but I'm worried about asking my boss for a pay rise in case she says no.
   B: Well, that's silly. ……… + ………

Spelling

Suffixes

① Each of these sentences contains a word that is spelled incorrectly. Underline the word and write its correct spelling at the end of the sentence.

1 We're very <u>gratful</u> for all the help you've given us. *grateful*

2 I woke up in the middle of the night, and thought I heard someone creepping slowly up the stairs. ………

3 When you go climbing, it's important that you have all the right equipement. ………

4 We were all surprised by his unexpected appearance at the party. ………

5 We hope that the experiment will be a success and that it will provide us with some usefull data. ………

6 Teachers should avoid discussing culturaly sensitive issues in class. ………

7 A person's happyness can depend on many different factors. ………

8 Planing a holiday or trip is sometimes much more enjoyable than the trip itself. ………

9 The television debate turned into a big arguement about whether or not humans are responsible for global warming. ………

10 Parents should be responsible for making sure their children's school attendence record is good. ………

Unit 7 Literacy skills

Listening
Form completion

❶ You are going to hear a man on the telephone booking some tickets for a book fair. Before you listen, look at Questions 1–7 and answer the question below.

Questions 1–7

Complete the form below.

Write NO MORE THAN TWO WORDS AND/OR A NUMBER for each answer.

International Book Fair
Ticket Booking Form

First name:	Angus
Last name:	1 ....
Address:	2 ...., Wallington, Oxford
Postcode:	3 ....
Phone number:	Home: 4 ....
5 ....:	0872 298 1191 (Between 9 a.m. and
6 .... p.m.)	
Date of visit:	7 .... 7th

What do you think you will need to complete each question? Choose an option, a–e, from the box. You may choose one option more than once.

a a word only   b a number only
c a number and two words   d two words
e a combination of letters and numbers

Question 1 ....   Question 5 ....
Question 2 ....   Question 6 ....
Question 3 ....   Question 7 ....
Question 4 ....

❷ 🔊 Now listen to the first part of the conversation and answer Questions 1–7.

Multiple choice

❸ Read Questions 8–12 quickly, and <u>underline</u> the key words in the first line of each question.

Questions 8–12

Choose the correct letter, **A**, **B** *or* **C**.

8 How will the woman send the man's tickets?
 A by email
 B by post
 C by text message

9 The author Sandra Harrington will
 A tell people about her latest book.
 B read extracts from one of her earlier books.
 C explain where writers get their ideas from.

10 To go to one of the author talks, the man must
 A reserve some tickets online before he goes.
 B buy tickets from the Book Fair office.
 C complete a form which the woman will send to him.

11 How will the man get to the fair from the city centre?
 A by car
 B on foot
 C by public transport

12 The woman says that the cafés and restaurants at the Book Fair are
 A very good.
 B extremely expensive.
 C better than other places in the area.

4 🔊 **Now listen to the next part of the conversation and answer Questions 8–12.**

Vocabulary

raise or *rise*?

1 <u>Underline</u> the correct word in these sentences.

1 The number of visitors has *risen / raised* by 20% this year.
2 When the college *rose / raised* its fees last year, the number of new students fell.
3 I asked my boss if he could *rise / raise* my salary.
4 The wind *rose / raised* in the night, and blew lots of trees down.

2 Complete these sentences with the correct form of *raise* or *rise*.

1 He ......*raised*...... his eyebrows in surprise when he heard the news.
2 Sales of electronic books have .... by 12% a month in the last year.
3 Please .... your hand if you want to ask a question.
4 We sat on the beach early in the morning and watched the sun as it ....
5 Book prices are .... by about 5% a year.
6 When the government .... taxes on books and magazines, a lot of people worried about the future of publishing.
7 He was sitting down when I entered the room, but he .... to shake my hand.
8 As we stood by the side of the river, we realised that the water level was .... rapidly.
9 I had to .... my voice to make myself heard over the noise.
10 One of the government's main aims in the next five years is to .... the level of literacy among the poor.

Key vocabulary

3 Arrange the letters in bold in these sentences to make words. The first and last letters of each word are in their correct place.

1 Could you remind me to pick up some **bhecorurs** ...*brochures*... from the travel agency?
2 I'm under **psusrree** .... as I have to write a 10,000 word essay by Monday.
3 At the end of every academic year, **uoynelnmempt** .... rates rise as people leave school and start looking for work.
4 You might find something **oinlne** .... to help you with your project.
5 I've got to go to a **lrteuce** .... on economics this afternoon.
6 A: Did you learn anything at the lecture?
   B: Not really. The speaker gave us a brief **otnliue** .... of the main points and told us to find out more ourselves.
7 This year, the amount of college work I have to do has increased **dmlaltraicay** ....
8 A: According to an article I've just read, almost 5% of the adult population is **iitaterlle** ....
   B: That's shocking. Everybody should be able to read and write.
9 A: Have you managed to make any **pesrorgs** .... with your essay?
   B: Not really. None of the books I need are in the library.
10 A: Have you had any **fcebadek** .... from your tutor on the essay you wrote?
    B: Yes, he was very positive about it.

Literacy skills

Reading
Matching information

❶ **You are going to read an article about graphic novels. Look at the title and the subheading. Which of these sentences summarises what the passage will say?**

a Graphic novels are generally a good thing.

b Graphic novels are generally a bad thing.

Now quickly read through the passage to check your answer.

Graphic novels

People who think graphic novels are just comics with a different name should think again

A Graphic novels, as the name suggests, are books written and illustrated in the style of a comic book. The term graphic novel was first used in 1978 by author and artist Will Eisner to distinguish a comic novel he had written and illustrated from newspaper comic strips. He described graphic novels as consisting of 'sequential art' – a series of illustrations which, when viewed in order, tell a story.

B Although today's graphic novels are a recent phenomenon, this basic way of telling stories has been used in various forms for centuries. Early cave drawings, hieroglyphics and medieval tapestries are examples of this. The term graphic novel is now generally used to describe any book in a comic format that resembles a novel in length and narrative development.

C Many adults feel that graphic novels are not the type of reading material that will help young people become good readers. They believe that graphic novels are somehow a bad influence that prevent 'real' reading. In other words, they think that they are not 'real' books.

D However, many quality graphic novels are now being seen as a method of storytelling on the same level as novels, films or audio books. From originally appealing to a small following of enthusiasts, they are now being accepted by librarians and teachers as proper literature for children and young adults. The main advantages are that they promote literacy, and attract and motivate young people to read.

E How do we know this? In the last few years, teachers and school libraries have reported outstanding success getting children to read with graphic novels. Many have mentioned the motivational factor of the graphic novel. This has been especially true with children who are usually reluctant to read, especially boys. The colourful pictures attract them, and then encourage them to find out what the story is about. Providing young people of all abilities with a wide range of reading materials, including graphic novels, can help them become lifelong readers.

F Furthermore, one of the main benefits of a graphic novel is that it can help students who are learning a foreign language, and who are having problems improving their reading skills. This is because the pictures provide clues to the meaning of the words. Language learners are therefore more motivated by graphic novels, and will acquire new vocabulary more quickly.

G Many teachers have reported great success when they have used graphic novels with their students, especially in the areas of English, social studies and art. They have discovered that, just like traditional forms of literature, they can be useful tools for helping students examine aspects of history, science, literature and art.

H The idea that graphic novels are too simple to be regarded as serious reading is no longer valid. The excellent graphic novels available today demand many of the same skills that are needed to understand traditional works of fiction. Often they actually contain more sophisticated vocabulary than traditional books. Reading them can help students develop the skills that are necessary to read more challenging works.

❷ **Now look at these questions, and underline the key words in each one. Then answer Questions 1–7.**

Questions 1–7
The Reading passage has eight paragraphs, **A–H**.
Which paragraph contains the following information?
*Write the correct letter, **A–H**.*

NB *You may use any letter more than once.*

1 people with negative attitudes towards graphic novels ....

2 a variety of school subjects where graphic novels can play an important role ....

3 why a graphic novel's visual element speeds up learning ....

4 a modern definition of graphic novels ....

5 graphic novels are as good as any other method of telling a story ....

6 graphic novels sometimes use advanced words ....

7 the historical use of pictures as a method of storytelling ....

Table completion

❸ Read the instructions for Questions 7–13 and the title of the table. Answer the questions below.

Questions 7–13

Complete the table below.

*Choose **NO MORE THAN TWO WORDS** from the passage for each answer.*

The advantages of graphic novels

Advantages	Who benefits?	How it works
They provide motivation to read.	7 .... readers	They are attracted by 8 .... This encourages them to find out what happens in the 9 ....
They help improve a student's 10	11 .... learners	The pictures act as visual 12 .... The student develops a larger 13 ....

1 Which three paragraphs contain the information you need?
   Paragraph .... introduces the subject.
   Paragraph .... and paragraph .... contain the information itself.

2 What is the maximum number of words you can write in each gap? ....

3 Can you answer using your own words? ....

❹ Now answer Questions 7–13. Use the words around each question to help you find the answers.

Writing

Task 1

❶ Look at the graph below, and complete sentences 1–8 with words and phrases from the box. There are two words or phrases that you do not need.

Borderline bookshop

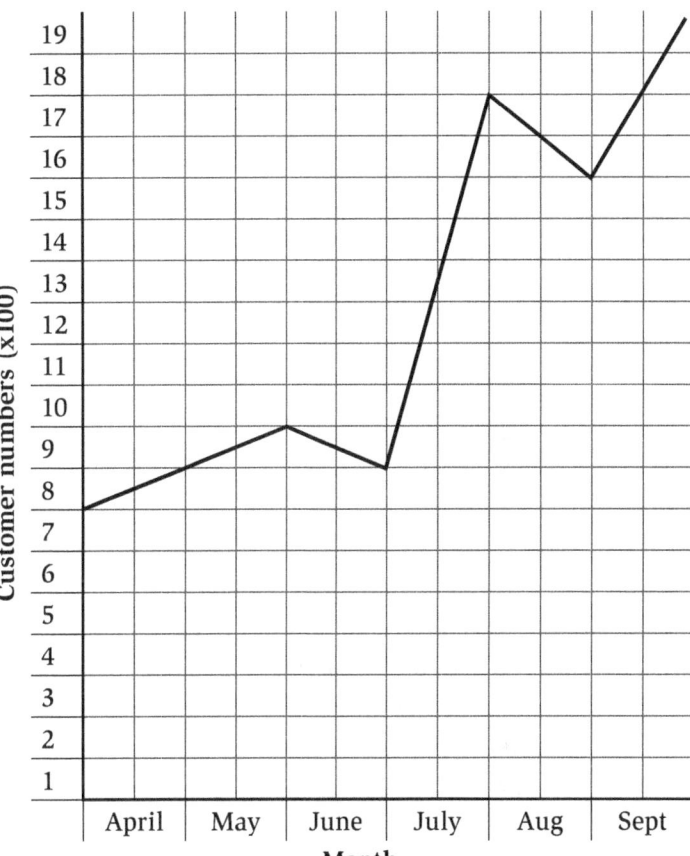

decreased slightly	downward trend	fell again
fluctuations	increased slightly	~~number~~	peaked
rose sharply	steady trend	upward trend

1 The graph shows the ......*number*...... of customers visiting a bookshop over a six-month period.

2 Customer numbers .... in May.

3 Customer numbers .... the following month.

4 Customer numbers .... in July.

5 Customer numbers .... in August.

6 Customer numbers .... in September.

7 There were .... in customer numbers between April and September.

8 The graph shows an .... generally.

Literacy skills 45

2 Complete the second sentence in each pair, replacing the words and phrases in bold with words from the box. You will need to use some words than once.

about	another	decrease	fall	fluctuated
gives	increase	information	peak	reached
rise	sharp	slight		

1 The graph **shows** the number of customers visiting a bookshop over a six-month period.
The graph ...*gives information about*... the number of customers visiting a bookshop over a six-month period.

2 Customer numbers **increased slightly** in May.
There was a .... in customer numbers in May.

3 Customer numbers **decreased slightly** the following month.
There was a .... in customer numbers the following month.

4 Customer numbers **rose sharply** in July.
There was a .... in customer numbers in July.

5 Customer numbers **fell again** in August.
There was .... in customer numbers in August.

6 Customer numbers **peaked** in September.
Customer numbers .... a .... in September.

7 There were **fluctuations** in customer numbers during the six-month period.
Customer numbers .... during the six-month period.

3 Look at the Writing task below, then do the exercises which follow it.

The graph below shows how much money a city council gave to book clubs over a four-year period.

Summarise the information by selecting and reporting the main features, and make comparisons where relevant.

You should write at least 150 words.

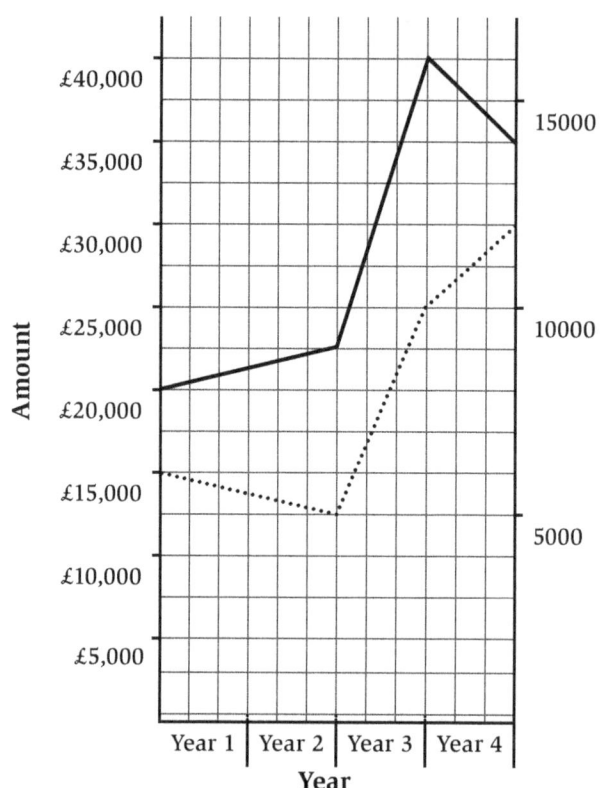

Council donations to book clubs

———— = Amount of money given
············ = Number of book club members

4 Are these sentences True or False? <u>Underline</u> your answers.

1 The graph shows how much money a city council received from book clubs in the city. True / False

2 The graph also shows how many book club members there were in the city. True / False

3 The graph covers a period of time that began and ended in the past. True / False

4 Over the four-year period, there was a steady rise in the amount of money that was given. True / False

5 Over the same period, the number of book club members fluctuated. True / False

6 Generally, there was a downward trend in the number of book club members. True / False

5 Now do the Writing task in Exercise 3. Try to use some of the words, phrases and structures from Exercises 1–4. You should write at least 150 words.

46 Unit 7

Grammar

Prepositions to describe graphs

1 Look at the graph and complete the paragraph with the prepositions from the box. In some cases, more than one preposition may be possible.

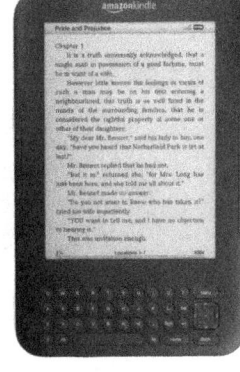

Mr Widget's Gadget Store
Ebook reader sales, 2011

| between | during | in | for | from | over |

The graph shows ebook reader sales for a small electronics company **1** ……………… a one-year period. Sales rose **2** ……………… January and March. Then they fell **3** ……………… April to June. They went up again **4** ……………… the summer, but fell again **5** ……………… October. They continued falling **6** ……………… the last two months of the year. Overall, ebook reader sales fluctuated considerably **7** ……………… 2011.

2 Complete sentences 1–5 using the information in the graph and the prepositions from the box.

| at | by | from | in | of | to |

January–March.

1 There was a rise ……………… sales of ebook readers.
2 Sales of ebook readers saw an increase ……………… 100%

April–June.

3 Sales fell ……………… 20.

July–September

4 Sales of readers rose ……………… 90 a month ……………… 130 a month.
5 Sales peaked ……………… 130.

Spelling

Forming adverbs from adjectives

Complete these sentences with an adverb form of the adjectives in brackets.

1 Nobody will understand you unless you speak more ..*clearly*.. (clear).
2 Some books are ……………… (incredible) expensive.
3 I'm sorry, but I've ……………… (accident) broken your camera.
4 It's ……………… (extreme) hard to concentrate with so much noise going on.
5 She stared at me ……………… (angry) and left the room.
6 We've studied your figures ……………… (careful) and can't find any mistakes.
7 When we discovered what the problem was, we ……………… (hasty) organised a meeting to deal with it.
8 The door opens ……………… (automatic) as you approach it.
9 If we think about the problem ……………… (logical), I'm sure we'll find a solution.
10 He looked at me ……………… (sympathetic) and shook his head.

Literacy skills

Unit 8 Tourist attractions

Reading

Summary completion

1 You are going to read a passage about tribal tourism. Look at the title and subheading. What do you think the passage will say about tribal tourism? Tick (✓) any of these sentences that you think apply.

a Tribal tourism holidays are not the same as other types of holiday. ☐
b Tribal tourism involves meeting local people. ☐
c Tribal tourism is dangerous. ☐
d More and more people are going on tribal holidays. ☐
e Tribal tourism has its disadvantages for some people. ☐
f Tribal holidays are very expensive. ☐

2 Read the passage quickly, and check your answers to Exercise 1.

Holidays with a difference

Tribal tourism is becoming more popular. But at what cost to the locals?

Tribal tourism is a relatively new type of tourism. It involves travellers going to remote destinations, staying with local people and learning about their culture and way of life. They stay in local accommodation, share facilities with local people, and join in with meals and celebrations. At the moment, less than one percent of holidays are tribal tourism holidays, but this is set to change.

Tribal tourism is often compared with foreign exchange visits. However, a foreign exchange involves staying with people who often share the same values. Tribal tourism takes visitors to places where the lifestyle is very different from that in their home location. Those who have been on a tribal holiday explain that experiencing this lifestyle is the main attraction. They say that it offers them the chance to live in a way they never have before.

Not everyone is convinced that tribal tourism is a good thing, and opinions are divided. The argument is about whether or not it helps the local population, or whether it exploits them. The main problem is that, because tribal tourism is relatively new, the long-term effects on local populations have not been studied in much detail. Where studies have been carried out, the effects have been found to be negative.

Travel writer Ian Coleman recalls a recent trip to Guatemala, where he saw an example of this. 'There is a village with a statue of a man called Maximon, who has a special spiritual meaning for the local tribe,' he explains. 'The statue is kept indoors, and once a year the locals bring him out and carry him around the village. However, visitors now pay money for them to bring the statue out and carry it around, while they take photographs. As a result, Maximon has lost his original meaning, and is now just another tourist attraction.'

So, is it possible to experience an exotic culture without harming it in some way? 'With a bit of thought, we can maximise the positive impacts and minimise the negative,' says travel company director Hilary Waterhouse. 'Remember that you are there not only to experience a different culture, but to help it in some way. Tourists bring money to the community, which the community can invest in local projects. However, this does not mean you can act the way you might do back home. The most important thing is to show respect, learn about, and be aware of, local customs and traditions. Always remember you're a guest.'

Dawn Baker, manager of travel company Footprints, runs tours to tribal areas in Peru. 'Good companies specialising in tribal tours are very careful about who they allow on their tours,' she says. 'They won't take anyone they feel is unsuitable.' Baker offers reading recommendations so that visitors can read about the country and its cultures. 'The rewards of a trip to this country are priceless, and the more you know in advance, the more priceless they are.'

Tribal tourism travellers are often surprised at how basic their facilities are when they get there. 'It's not for everyone, but for me it was all part of the experience,' says Jamie White, who has recently returned from a trip to Borneo. 'We stayed in the same huts that everyone was living in, with no running water and no electricity. It was basic, but it was an ethical way to travel. Being comfortable means you use more local resources and so have more of an environmental impact.'

3 Read the summary in Exercise 4.

1 Decide what type of information you need for each gap.
2 Find the paragraphs in the passage where you will find the information you need.

4 Now answer Questions 1–8.

Questions 1–8
Complete the summary below.

Choose **NO MORE THAN TWO WORDS AND/OR A NUMBER** *from the passage for each answer.*

Tribal tourism

People who take a tribal tourism holiday visit places that are **1** .... When they are there, they find out about the local **2** .... and how people live. Currently, tribal tourism accounts for less than **3** .... of the tourism industry.

Tribal tourism holidays are different from foreign exchange visits because the travellers and the people they meet have different **4** .... Tribal tourism travellers experience a **5** .... that they are not familiar with. For them, this is its **6** .... However, some people argue that **7** .... do not benefit from this kind of tourism. **8** .... show that the effects of tribal tourism are not good.

Matching features

5 The passage contains the names of four people.

1 Find their names and <u>underline</u> them.
2 <u>Underline</u> the key words in this statement.
   'Some people may be refused a place on a tribal tour.'
3 Now match the statement with the person who says something which has the same meaning in the passage. Complete this sentence with the person's name:
   The statement can be matched with ....
4 How do you know this is the correct answer? <u>Underline</u> the sentence or sentences in the passage that give you this information.

6 Now <u>underline</u> the key words in statements 9–13 in Exercise 7.

7 Answer the questions by reading around each name in the passage carefully and then read the list of statements to find the ones that match. Write the correct letter A–D after each statement.

Questions 9–13

Look at the following statements and the list of people below.

Match each statement with the correct person, **A–D**.

NB *You may use any letter more than once.*

9 Travellers may need to change the way they behave. ....
10 Some travellers would not enjoy living the way that the local people do. ....
11 Tribal tourism can have benefits for local people. ....
12 Some travellers make local people do things that they would not normally do. ....
13 Learning about a place before you go there makes your trip much more satisfying. ....

List of People
A Ian Coleman
B Hilary Waterhouse
C Dawn Baker
D Jamie White

Vocabulary

tourism or *tourist*?

1 Complete these sentences using *tourism*, *tourist* or *tourists*.

1 Tribal .... is becoming more popular.
2 Hotel prices can double during the .... season.
3 .... numbers in the region have increased dramatically in the last two years.
4 .... is relatively new in my city.
5 Many people believe that mass .... is responsible for a lot of environmental problems.
6 There are no longer enough hotels to deal with the huge number of .... who visit the city.

Tourist attractions

Key vocabulary

2 Complete each passage with words or phrases from the boxes.

A holiday to forget?
Part 1

aircraft	capable	delay	magical
memorable	package deal		sightseeing
stressful	tour guide	vacation	

The first two days of my holiday last year were **1** .... , but for all the wrong reasons. I had seen an advertisement for a **2** .... in the newspaper. It said 'Enjoy a **3** .... two-week **4** .... tour around the Parakeet Islands, accompanied by a qualified, experienced **5** .... '. As I really needed a **6** .... and had never visited the region, I decided to go. Things got off to a bad start at the airport when there was a seven-hour **7** .... for the flight. When the **8** .... finally arrived, I almost decided not to get on it. It was ancient, and I really didn't think it would be **9** .... of getting us there. I was beginning to find the whole thing a bit **10** ....

Part 2

abroad	breathtaking	continent	evidence
leisure activities	monuments		outdated
resort	urban	within reach	

The flight to the Parakeet Islands took 26 hours, and I think we must have landed in every **11** .... except Antarctica on the way there! We eventually reached the **12** .... where we were going to stay for our first two nights. I must admit that the view of the beach from my window was **13** .... , we were **14** .... of several restaurants, and a lot of **15** .... , such as sailing and beach volleyball, were available on the beach. There were also some interesting-looking historical **16** .... in the area. Unfortunately, we were also close to a large, busy **17** .... area, which meant it was quite noisy. Secondly, the rooms were small and the furniture was scruffy and **18** .... Most worrying, however, there was **19** .... of mice under the beds. I know that things are different **20** .... , but I don't think *anyone* would have found this acceptable.

Listening
Sentence completion

1 Read Questions 1–6. Then match the type of information that you need, a–h, with Questions 1–6. There are two types of information that you do not need.

Questions 1–6

Complete the sentences below.

*Write **NO MORE THAN TWO WORDS AND/OR A NUMBER** for each answer.*

1 Make sure you get on .... at the beginning and end of the trip.
2 Go to the .... if you get separated from the guide.
3 The .... card entitles you to a discount on food and drink in the palace.
4 Get permission from the locals before taking their ....
5 Local people will accept .... less than the price they have asked for souvenirs.
6 Avoid .... the statue of King Hupugarta.

a an amount of money ....
b a person's job ....
c a form of transport ....
d something you create with a camera ....
e a meeting place ....
f something that you should see ....
g something you should not do ....
h you will pay less if you use this when you buy something ....

2 🎧 Now listen and answer Questions 1–6.

Table completion

❸ You are going to hear the next part of the guide's talk. Before you do this, look at the table. Then answer Questions 1 and 2 below.

Questions 7–14

Complete the table below.

Write NO MORE THAN ONE WORD AND/OR A NUMBER for each answer.

Palace of Kom Ombane

main attractions	when built or opened	what you will see
Statue of King Hupugarta in 7 .... Court	123 BCE	Statue of king covered in real 8 ....
Temple of the Sun	About 9 .... ago	Many columns, some as high as 10 ....
11 .... Chambers in the New Palace	1346	Private rooms of the kings and queens
The palace 12	13	Collection of jewellery, 14 .... and other historical objects

1 *Without* listening to the talk, can you explain why these answers to 7, 8 and 9 could *NOT* be correct?
 - Statue of King Hupugarta in **7** *the Central* Court
 - Statue of king covered in real **8** *silver and jewels*
 - **9** *1000 or 1100 years* ago
 ....

2 Can you explain why these answers could not be correct either?
 - Statue of King Hupugarta in **7** *some* Court
 - Statue of king covered in real **8** *expensive*
 - **9** *100* ago.
 ....

❹ 🔊 Now listen and answer Questions 7–14.

Writing

Task 2

❶ Read this Writing task and underline the key ideas.

Write about the following topic.

Some people say that travel helps us to appreciate other cultures.

How true is this statement? Do you think that people who travel a lot appreciate other cultures more than those who stay at home?

Give reasons for your answers and include any relevant examples from your own experience.

Write at least 250 words.

❷ Are these statements about the Writing task in Exercise 1 true (T) or false (F)?

1 The main topic is about what other cultures are like. ....

2 I must say whether or not I agree with the statement. ....

3 I must talk about the benefits of staying at home. ....

4 I should say why I have a certain opinion about the subject. ....

5 I should support my ideas with reasons and examples. ....

6 I should write in detail about a holiday or trip I have taken. ....

7 I can write more than 250 words. ....

3 Here are the first three paragraphs (introduction and two body paragraphs) from a sample answer. Match the first part of each paragraph, 1–3, with its second part, A–C.

1 **Introduction** ....

Before mass tourism made overseas travel available to everyone, people were rather ignorant of the world beyond their homes. For many, this changed when they began to travel.

2 **First main paragraph** ....

However, for others, their views remained unchanged. One reason for this was that they did not actually *experience* the culture of the country they were visiting. In many cases, this was because they were not interested in it.

3 **Second main paragraph** ....

Unfortunately, this is still true today. In my country, the main reason many people go abroad is to get a suntan and go swimming in the sea. They show little interest in the local people or their way of life.

A They simply wanted to go somewhere where they could relax and enjoy some warm weather. In other cases, they found the thought of experiencing the culture a frightening prospect, especially if it was very different from their own.

B Consequently, they learn no more about the country they are in than people who stay at home. A recent survey of holidaymakers indicates that 76% did not leave their hotel or resort unless they went on a guided tour.

C They learnt a lot about other cultures, and benefited from personally experiencing them. As a result, they returned home having a much greater appreciation and understanding of other cultures.

4 The sample answer above has no conclusion. Choose the best conclusion from the four below.

The best conclusion is ....

A I believe, therefore, that everyone who travels learns something about the local culture. They do not even have to leave their hotel to do this. They can learn as much about the local people and their way of life by just sitting on the beach as they can by going out and exploring.

B In my view, those who stay at home probably learn much more about foreign cultures than those who travel. This is because they can do it in an environment that they feel comfortable in. It is no longer necessary to travel in order to learn about the world.

C In my opinion, therefore, travel *can* help us to appreciate other cultures. However, we need to make an effort to do so, and this involves leaving the comfort of our hotel and going into the community. Unfortunately, it seems that too few people are prepared to do this.

D In conclusion, not everyone who travels appreciates the local culture. Another reason for this may be that they do not want to experience anything that is unfamiliar. They want things to be the way that they are in their home country, except with better weather.

5 Now write your answer to this Writing task. You might find some of the language in Exercises 2–4 helpful. You should write at least 250 words.

> Write about the following topic.
>
> *Some people say that you can learn more about another country by watching television programmes and films about it than by actually visiting it.*
>
> *How true is this statement? Is there anything you can learn about another country by visiting it that you cannot learn by watching programmes and films about it?*
>
> Give reasons for your answers and include any relevant examples from your own experience.

Grammar

Relative pronouns: *who, which, that, where*

1 Write these sentence pairs as one sentence, using a relative pronoun to join them together. Remember to remove any unnecessary words.

1 Football is a popular sport. It is played all over the world.
   Football is a popular sport that / which is played all over the world

2 There's a man in my town. He can remember the name of everyone he's ever met.
   ....
   ....

3 *Perfume* is a famous novel. I've read it many times.
   ....
   ....

4 There's a tourist information office in the town centre. You can get all the information you need there.

....

....

5 There's a tortoise in the zoo. It is over 150 years old.

....

....

6 *The Angry Olive* is an excellent restaurant. You can eat there for less than £10.

....

....

❷ **The relative pronouns have been left out of these sentences. Correct them by writing *who*, *which* or *that* in the correct place.**

1 I spent two weeks on an island ∧ is famous for its wildlife.   *that/which*

2 I'm not sure people travel a lot learn more about the world.

3 New York is the city I'd most like to live.

4 To get to Oxford, take the train leaves from platform 18.

5 Most tourists visit my country rarely explore the countryside.

6 If you visit my city, I can recommend several places might interest you.

7 On the island, there were birds would eat right out of your hand.

8 There aren't many places left in the country you can get away from the crowds of tourists.

❸ **In which of these sentences can we omit the relative pronoun? Tick (✓) the relevant boxes.**

1 The man <u>who</u> we met last night seemed very friendly. ✓

2 The book <u>that</u> you lent me wasn't very interesting. ☐

3 I met a man <u>who</u> says he can get tickets for the show tonight. ☐

4 There aren't many people <u>who</u> I know in the town. ☐

5 I know of several people <u>who</u> have never been abroad. ☐

6 There are several bus services <u>which</u> can get you into the city centre. ☐

7 My cousin Andy is someone <u>who</u> I really look up to. ☐

8 Here's the money <u>which</u> you asked me for. ☐

9 My brother has only two faults: everything that he says and everything <u>that</u> he does. ☐

10 The woman <u>who</u> runs the tourist information office is very helpful. ☐

Spelling

Introductory and linking phrases

There are ten spelling mistakes in this passage. <u>Underline</u> the incorrect words and write the correct spelling below.

At the beginning of the last <u>centry</u>, people did not have as many holidays as they do now, and althought companies specialising in foreign travel existed, their customers only formed a tiny percentage of the travelling public. Nowdays it seems that everybody travels abroad for their holidays, and the world is changing as a result. Therfore, we need to ask ourselves if this is a good thing or a bad thing.

Unfortunately, I believe that mass tourism is not such a good thing. A place that has become a popular tourist destination sometime benefits, since more jobs are created for local people. However, there are also disadvantages. First of all, there are environmental probelms, since more tourists mean more pollution. Secondly, small, independent businesses struggle to compete against big companies and hotel chains that move into the area. Finaly, partly as a result of the second point above, a place that becomes popular with tourists is at risk of losing its unique cultural identity.

In conclucion, it would be fair to say that overseas travel is fun, interesting and exciting for the traveller, but in my oppinion there is usually a price to pay for the place they are visiting.

1 *century*
2 ....
3 ....
4 ....
5 ....
6 ....
7 ....
8 ....
9 ....
10 ....

Unit 9 **Every drop counts**

Listening

Matching

1 This diagram shows a process known as cloud seeding. What do you think this is?

a how clouds prevent modern weapons from working properly
b how modern weapons can be used to produce rain
c how modern weapons behave when they enter thick cloud

2 [20] You are going to hear a student talking to her tutor about an essay she has written on controlling the weather. Now listen to the first part of the conversation and answer Questions 1–5.

Questions 1–5

What comment does the tutor make about each part of the student's essay?

Write the correct letter, A–C, next to Questions 1–5.

NB *You may use any letter more than once.*

Essay parts

1 the introduction
2 the description of problems caused by the weather
3 the section on weather-control programmes
4 the description of cloud seeding
5 the conclusion

Comments

A It is not well organised.
B It contains information that is not, or may not be, correct.
C It contains information that is not relevant.

Flow-chart completion

3 Read through the flow chart below, and decide what type of word you need for Questions 6–10.

Questions 6–10

Complete the flow chart below.

Write **NO MORE THAN TWO WORDS** *for each answer.*

Cloud seeding

The chemical silver iodide is introduced into a cloud by a rocket or by **6** ....

This causes tiny water drops in the cloud to **7** ...., in a process called static seeding.

Lots of very small pieces of **8** .... join together in a process called riming.

These fall from the sky, turning to rain or snow.

A secondary effect, known as dynamic seeding, occurs when water that freezes **9** ....

Sometimes this can cause the clouds to grow larger and **10** ....

4 [21] Now listen to the conversation, and answer Questions 6–10.

Unit 9

Reading

Matching headings

❶ You are going to read a typical IELTS Reading passage. Before you read the whole passage, look at the title, subheading and first paragraph. What do you think the rest of the passage will be about? Choose one or more from the list below.

1 a description of farming techniques in China ☐
2 what happens when farms don't get enough rain ☐
3 whether or not cloud seeding is a good way of creating rain ☐
4 research to test how effective cloud seeding is ☐
5 a general description of how cloud seeding is being carried out in one or more places ☐
6 a detailed scientific description of how cloud seeding works ☐
7 the possible advantages and disadvantages of cloud seeding ☐

The rain makers

Science and technology work with nature to bring rain when and where it is needed

A Wheat farmer Gang Liu is a worried man. The annual rains have not arrived, and there is a danger that unless there is substantial rainfall soon, his annual wheat crop will fail. As he looks anxiously at the clouds which promise rain but are failing to deliver it, there is a sudden loud roar, and from fields for miles around, hundreds of small rockets are fired into the clouds. Within twenty minutes, the farms around the eastern Chinese city of Luohe are experiencing their first rain for many weeks. Gang Liu's valuable wheat has been saved, thanks to a technique known as 'cloud seeding', in which the chemical silver iodide (AgI) is introduced into clouds. This causes the tiny drops of moisture in the clouds to turn to ice. These tiny ice particles join until they become heavy enough to fall from the sky, turning into rain as they melt.

B But did cloud seeding really cause the rain in Luohe to fall, or was it just a coincidence? Experts often question whether cloud seeding actually works. It is hard to tell how effective cloud seeding actually is, they say, as it might have rained anyway, without human intervention. But this has not stopped many governments and organisations from trying. There are currently 150 weather-modifying projects taking place in more than 40 countries. Not all of them are aimed at creating rain. The Eastlund Scientific Enterprises Corporation in the USA, for example, is experimenting with firing microwaves into clouds to prevent the tornadoes which cause enormous damage to the country every year. In Russia, experiments have been carried out to make sure the sun shines during important national events.

C However, it is rainmaking that dominates the research programmes. In many of these, researchers are using trials in which some clouds are 'seeded' while others are not, and both groups are monitored. Arlen Huggins of the Desert Research Institute is leading a research project in Australia. Weather-monitoring technology is so good nowadays, he says, that we can measure clouds much more effectively, even from the inside. As a result, we now know much more about the effect humans can have on the weather. What Huggins' team has discovered so far is promising. They believe that cloud seeding does work, although there are still two years of the six-year project left to go.

D In China, where the majority of cloud-seeding operations take place, weather-modification authorities use army rockets to fire silver-iodide particles into the clouds. 39,000 staff working for the China Meteorological Administration (CMA) are equipped with 7,113 army cannons which, in 2006, were used to fire a million silver-iodide rockets into the atmosphere. This costs over $100 million a year, although the CMA claims the results are worth the expense. Between 1999 and 2006, they say, cloud seeding produced 250 billion metric tonnes of rain and prevented thousands of farmers from losing their crops.

E "We want to understand what makes clouds rain," says Philip Brown of the UK Meteorological office, explaining why so much time, effort and money are being invested. "But there is a more powerful economic reason. A lot of countries around the world are at risk from drought, and governments will try anything to make sure that doesn't happen, even if the scientific evidence is weak. The potential economic value is greater than the scientific value. Making it rain might allow you to keep agriculture going where, without human intervention, it might fail."

F Some people are concerned, however, that altering the weather can have negative consequences. Leonard Barrie, director of the research department at the World Meteorological Organisation in Geneva, explains why. "All areas of weather modification are still very controversial. Some people think that diverting water for irrigation benefits some people, but is a disadvantage to others. Someone in one area will get more water, but as a result, someone somewhere else could get less." His fears may be justified. Recently, the town of Zhoukou in China's Henan province accused neighbouring town Pingdingshang of 'stealing' rain from clouds that were due to pass over its own farms, prompting what may be the world's very first documented incident of 'rain rage'.

❷ Now check your answers to Exercise 1 by quickly reading the rest of the passage.

3 Now look at the Reading task below. Before you do the task, use a dictionary to check the meanings of the underlined words in i–ix.

> **Questions 1–6**
>
> *The reading passage has six paragraphs, **A–F**.*
>
> *Choose the correct heading for each paragraph from the list of headings below.*
>
> **List of headings**
>
> i   Making peaceful use of a military weapon
> ii How modifying the weather has changed the world
> iii What is prompting this research?
> iv A period of drought comes to an end
> v   An old solution to a new problem
> vi Winners and losers
> vii Tests provide encouraging results
> viii A waste of money
> ix Global attempts to change the weather
>
> | 1 Paragraph A .... | 4 Paragraph D .... |
> | 2 Paragraph B .... | 5 Paragraph E .... |
> | 3 Paragraph C .... | 6 Paragraph F .... |

4 Now read each paragraph carefully and match it to the correct heading.

Sentence completion

5 Read the task and Questions 7–12 below. Then answer these questions.

1 How many words can you write in each answer?
   ....

2 How many numbers can you write in each answer? ....

3 Can you write a word *and* a number in each answer? ....

4 Look at the sentences and decide which of these types of word could *not* be used to complete any of the sentences. Tick (✓) one or more word types.

   a noun   ☐   a verb   ☐
   an adjective ☐   an adverb   ☐

> **Questions 7–12**
>
> *Complete the sentences below.*
>
> *Choose **NO MORE THAN ONE WORD AND/OR A NUMBER** from the passage for each answer.*
>
> 7 Experts are unsure if cloud seeding is .... or not.
> 8 At the moment, there are over .... where projects are being carried out to modify the weather.
> 9 Thanks to modern .... , it is now possible to get better results when clouds are monitored.
> 10 The Desert Research Institute project will finish in a couple of ....
> 11 The CMA gets the equipment they need from the ....
> 12 A large number of .... benefited from cloud seeding carried out by the CMA.

6 Now do Questions 7–12.

Pick from a list

7 Look at Questions 13–14 below and underline the key words. Use these to find the right places in the passage.

> **Questions 13–14**
>
> *Choose **TWO letters**, **A–E**.*
>
> *Which **TWO** of these sentences are true about cloud seeding, according to the passage?*
>
> A China carries out more cloud seeding than anywhere else.
> B Cloud seeding is too expensive for most countries.
> C Cloud seeding is mostly done for scientific rather than economic reasons.
> D Cloud seeding helps turn dry areas of land into agricultural areas.
> E Cloud seeding may affect the distribution of rainfall.

8 Now answer Questions 13–14.

Unit 9

Spelling

Some common mistakes

The following comes from the Reading passage. Each one contains a spelling mistake. <u>Underline</u> the word and write the correct spelling.

1 The <u>anual</u> rains have not arrived,... *annual*
2 Gang Liu's <u>valueble</u> wheat has been saved...
3 In Russia, <u>experriments</u> have been carried out...
4 What Huggins' team has discovered so far is promissing.
5 ... staff working for the CMA are equiped with 7,113 army cannons ...
6 Wheat farmer Gang Liu is a worryed man.
7 ... goverments will try anything to make sure that doesn't happen.
8 Experts often question wether cloud seeding actually works.

Vocabulary

effect, benefit, advantage, disadvantage

❶ **Complete the passage by <u>underlining</u> the best words.**

A new suburb has been planned for Bolingbroke. It will bring huge **1** <u>benefits</u> / *effects* to the city, by creating new housing and job opportunities. Unfortunately, there will also be some major **2** *advantages* / *disadvantages*. Above all, we must consider the negative **3** *benefit* / *effect* it will have on the environment. The most significant **4** *benefit* / *disadvantage* is that building the suburb means that a local nature reserve will have to be destroyed, which will have a significant **5** *benefit* / *effect* on wildlife in the area. Furthermore, this nature reserve has brought many **6** *advantage* / *benefits* to the people who live in the city, since it is a place where they can go to escape from the noise and traffic. They will no longer have this option. We also need to consider the serious **7** *advantage* / *effect* the new suburb will have on water supplies. One of the biggest **8** *effects* / *advantages* of the nature reserve is that it has a reservoir, which provides water to the city. When this goes, there will be less water for an even bigger population.

❷ **Complete these sentences with *for*, *of* or *on*.**

1 What are the advantages .... living in the countryside?
2 The heavy rain had a negative effect .... tourism in the area.
3 The nature reserve has huge benefits .... the local population.
4 The most significant disadvantage .... living near a river is the danger of flooding.
5 Everyone knows the benefits .... getting plenty of exercise.
6 We don't know the long-term effects .... climate change.

Key vocabulary

❸ **Complete the sentences with words and phrases from the box.**

<del>access</del>   construction   cultivate crops   irrigation
droughts   account for   geological
human consumption   hygiene   minerals   poured
rainwater   water supplies   water purification
water sports   wet suit

1 People need .....*access*..... to clean running water in order to maintain basic ....
2 Despite the dry climate, farmers can .... here, thanks to a modern .... system.
3 Contrary to popular belief, ... only .... a relatively small percentage of famines worldwide.
4 The water here is generally fit for ...., but we recommend adding .... tablets just to be sure.
5 For some ...., especially surfing, a .... is useful.
6 The roof was in such poor condition that every time there was a storm, ... through it into the house.
7 It is hoped that the .... of a new reservoir will improve .... to homes in the area.
8 A .... survey carried out in the area showed it to be rich in several valuable ....

Every drop counts 57

Writing

Task 1

1 Read the Writing task below and look at the diagram. Decide which information below goes in which box in the diagram. Write the appropriate number (1–8) in each box.

The diagram below shows a simple device for changing sea water to drinking water.

Summarise the information by selecting and reporting the main features, and make comparisons where relevant.

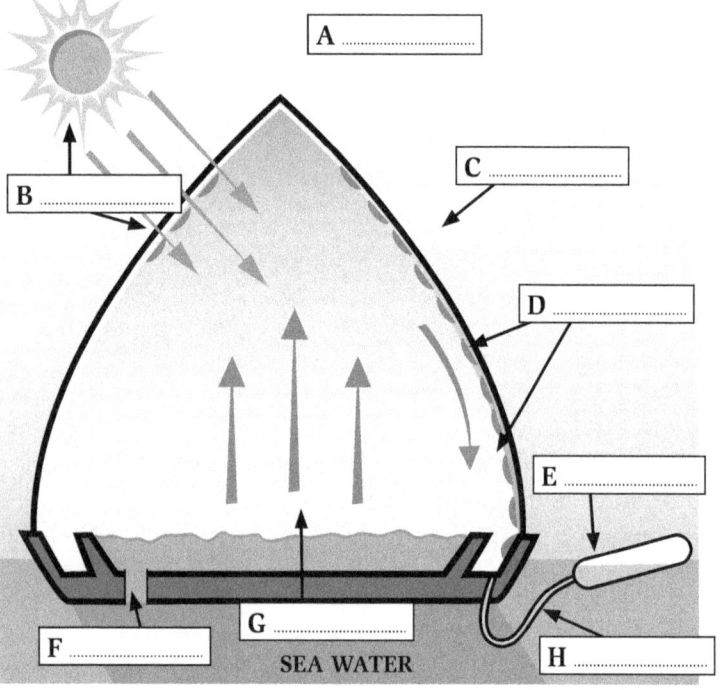

1 Evaporated water condenses on the dome and flows into rim.
2 Rubber tube.
3 Dome lets in sunlight.
4 How a floating solar still converts sea water to drinking water.
5 Drinking water collector.
6 Heat from sun's rays evaporates sea water.
7 Sea water enters through a small hole.
8 Plastic container with clear plastic dome.

2 What should each paragraph in the Writing task contain? Match the paragraphs (1–4) with the necessary information (a–f). There are two letters that you do *not* need.

1 Paragraph 1 should
2 Paragraph 2 should
3 Paragraph 3 should
4 Paragraph 4 should

a describe how well you think the device works.
b explain how the system works.
c explain how to set up the system.
d explain what the diagram shows and list the equipment.
e explain what sort of person would want one of these.
f contain an overview of the diagram.

3 Put sentences A–I in the correct order, and match with the paragraphs in Exercise 2.

.... A The larger plastic container is placed on the sea water, where it floats.

.... B The water flows down the dome into the rim of the container, through the rubber tube into the drinking water collector.

.... C Sunlight passes through the clear dome and heats up the sea water, which evaporates and condenses on the inside of the dome.

.... D The diagram shows how a bit of basic equipment can be used to produce clean drinking water in just a few simple steps.

.... E The distilled water collector is attached to the container by a rubber tube, and is placed in the water next to it.

.... F It is ready to drink.

...1... G The diagram shows a way in which sea water can be converted to drinking water using a simple device called a floating solar still.

.... H The process begins when the bottom of the larger container is partly filled by sea water, which enters through a small hole.

.... I This device consists of a clear plastic dome, a rubber tube and a smaller container called a distilled water collector.

❹ Now write your answer to the following Writing task. You should write at least 150 words.

The diagrams below show two methods of using water to produce electricity.

Summarise the information by selecting and reporting the main features, and make comparisons where relevant.

Hydroelectric dam

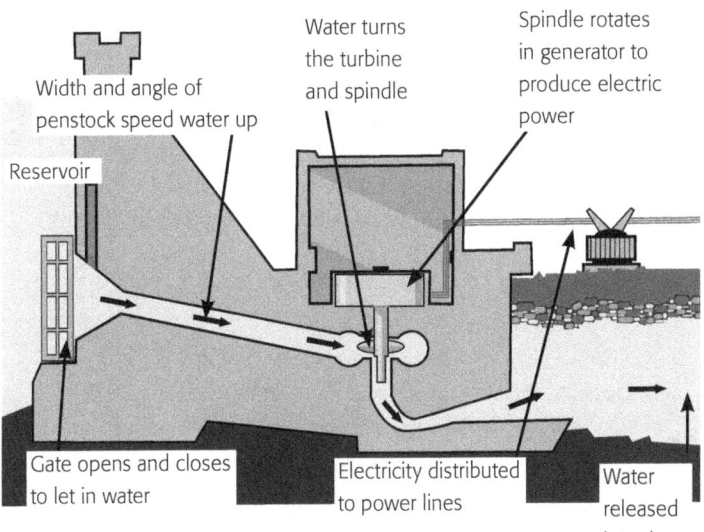

Wave-air generator

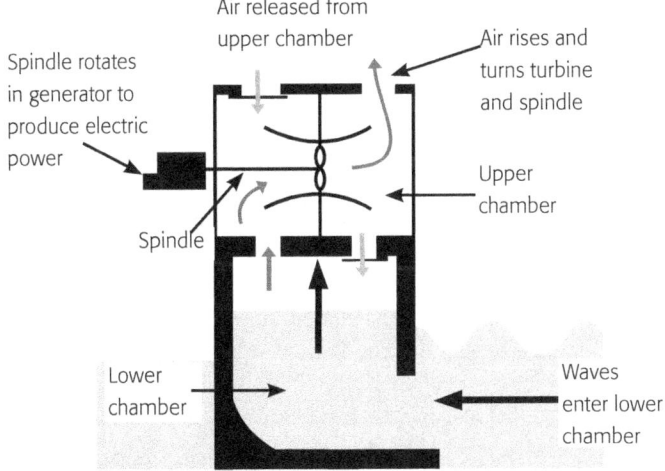

Grammar

The passive

❶ Complete the second sentence in each pair so that it is passive. Pay particular attention to the tense of the main verb.

1 People spend a lot of money on bottled water.
  A lot of money ...is spent... on bottled water.

2 A local celebrity opened the new swimming pool yesterday.
  The new swimming pool .... yesterday.

3 The recent bad weather has damaged the dam near the reservoir.
  The dam near the reservoir ....

4 We can use a solar still to convert sea water to drinking water.
  A solar still .... to convert sea water to drinking water.

5 The council will fine anyone who pollutes the lake.
  Anyone who pollutes the lake ....

6 Swimmers must wear swimming caps in the pool.
  Swimming caps .... in the pool.

Sequencers

❷ Improve this sample answer from the Writing section using the words from the box. In some cases, more than one answer may be possible, but you should try to use each word once only.

| finally | first | next | now | then |

The diagram shows a way in which sea water can be converted to drinking water using a simple device called a floating solar still. This device consists of a plastic container with a clear plastic dome, a rubber tube and a smaller container called a distilled water collector.

1 ...., the larger plastic container is placed on the surface of the sea water, where it floats.
2 ...., the distilled water collector is attached to the container by a rubber tube, and is placed in the water next to it.

The process begins when the bottom of the larger container is partly filled by sea water, which enters through a small hole in the side. Sunlight 3 .... passes through the clear dome and heats up the sea water, which evaporates and condenses on the inside of the dome. 4 ...., the water flows down the dome into the rim of the container, through the rubber tube into the drinking water collector. It is 5 .... ready to drink.

The diagram shows how a bit of basic equipment can be used to produce clean drinking water in just a few simple steps.

Every drop counts 59

Unit 10 Building design

Reading

Multiple choice

1 You are going to read a passage about a famous architect called Le Corbusier. Read the passage quickly then match the words (1–10), in bold in the passage, with their correct definition (a-j).

Word	Definition
1 brand-new	a completely different from what was done before
2 followers	b to be made to experience something (often something unpleasant)
3 enthusiastic	c uncovered or unprotected, and able to be seen by people
4 exposed	
5 exaggeration	d stopped following a plan, idea, etc.
	e very ugly
6 revolutionary	f showing a lot of interest in something
7 significant	g important because it is a reason why changes happened
8 abandoned	h completely new
9 hideous	i people who believe in a particular person or set of ideas
10 subjected to	j when you describe something as larger, better, worse, etc., than it actually is

The man who tried to destroy Paris

Le Corbusier was one of the most influential architects of the 20th century. But many may wish he had never built anything

Born Charles-Edouard Jeanneret in Switzerland in 1887, the architect Le Corbusier used his grandfather's name when he went to Paris at the age of 29. As Jeanneret, he had been a fairly successful small-town architect; as Le Corbusier, he had bigger ideas. He disliked the architectural styles that were popular at the time, and considered them to be out of date in an industrial age. He believed that the 20th century deserved a **brand-new** style of architecture. "We must start again from zero," he said.

The new style of architecture was called the International Style, and it attracted many **followers** in the architectural world. However, nobody was as **enthusiastic** about it as Le Corbusier at the beginning. He worked hard to promote his ideas at exhibitions, at talks, in books and in his own magazine. He loved machines, and believed that, like a machine, a building should have a function. He is famous for saying: "A house is a machine for living in."

The machines he admired the most were ships, and his early buildings tried to capture the spirit of the sea with their white walls, **exposed** rooms, shining glass and flat roofs. He called this style of architecture 'purism'. The first building to embrace this style was the Villa Savoye in France. Le Corbusier believed that it was one of the best, most functional houses ever built. Unfortunately, this turned out to be an **exaggeration**. The flat roof was a particular problem, as water poured in every time it rained, and it needed constant repairs. Nevertheless, its design was **revolutionary**, and it should be considered a **significant** piece of early 20th-century architecture.

In 1935, Le Corbusier visited New York City. He loved the city, and especially its tall buildings. He had only one reservation, which he explained to a journalist for the *Herald Tribune* newspaper. American skyscrapers were the biggest, tallest buildings in the world at that time, but Le Corbusier was a man who always thought big, and as far as he was concerned, they were "just too small". Le Corbusier had always admired tall buildings. Now, inspired by his visit, he **abandoned** purism. It is doubtful that he could have created anything as grand as the skyscrapers he had seen in the city, but from now on Le Corbusier started designing buildings that sent out a more powerful message.

He first started using bright colours, and then experimented with concrete. Le Corbusier loved the look and flexibility of concrete, and found it hard to hide it behind brick or paint, preferring to leave it on full view. At a time when concrete was seen as modern and exciting, his designs made him world famous, and he was asked to design several important buildings around the world. Altogether, he designed about 60 major buildings worldwide, in a style that became known as 'modernism'.

However, while many admired and copied his new style of architecture, many more hated it. They turned against him, and tried to block his plans. Buildings should inspire people and make them feel good, they said, and Le Corbusier's ugly, depressing buildings often had the opposite effect. In this respect, the people of Paris had a lucky escape. Early in his career, Le Corbusier had wanted to knock down the centre of Paris and replace the old buildings with huge towers. Fortunately, his plan was rejected. Justifiably, in view of his plans to transform one of the world's most beautiful cities into a **hideous** concrete jungle, Le Corbusier is still known as 'the man who tried to destroy Paris'.

Despite the criticism, he had an enormous effect on the world of architecture, and attracted a large number of followers. As a result, many places were **subjected to** his style. In the Paris suburbs of Bobigny, for example, huge towers were built to house some of the city's poorer inhabitants. Other European cities such as London, Berlin and Dublin also felt his influence.

Apart from the buildings that were directly influenced by Le Corbusier, something else happened that the architect never planned: there was a return to older styles of architecture. Today, many people live in modern houses that look like they are much older. This look may represent a return to traditional tastes and values. More likely, however, it represents a reaction against modernist architecture.

❷ Underline the key ideas in Questions 1–4. Then answer the questions.

Questions 1–4

Choose the correct letter, A, B, C or D.

1 What does the writer say about Le Corbusier in the first paragraph?
   A He had a relative who was also an architect.
   B He became successful when he went to Paris.
   C He thought that there were too many industrial buildings.
   D He wanted to do something different from everyone else.

2 What does the writer say about the International Style in the second paragraph?
   A A lot of other architects liked it.
   B At first, people did not like it very much.
   C It took a lot of hard work to get people to accept it.
   D The buildings looked like machines.

3 Why does the writer describe the Villa Savoye as 'revolutionary' in the third paragraph?
   A It looked more like a ship than a building.
   B Nobody had built anything like it before.
   C It looked nice, but had too many faults.
   D It was more functional than any other building of the time.

4 What is the writer's main purpose in the fourth paragraph?
   A to explain why Le Corbusier visited New York
   B to show that Le Corbusier was not impressed by New York's skyscrapers
   C to describe Le Corbusier's reaction to New York
   D to explain why Le Corbusier changed his style of architecture

Matching sentence endings

❸ Read Questions 5–8 and the endings A–F.

1 Underline the key words in the questions and use these to find the right place in the passage.
2 Read that part of the passage carefully and match the information to the key words in the endings.

Questions 5–8

Complete each sentence with the correct ending, A–F, below.

5 Le Corbusier's Villa Savoye
6 The concrete in Le Corbusier's later buildings
7 Le Corbusier's style of architecture
8 Le Corbusier had a large following which

A copied the style that he had invented.
B is a classic example of modernist architecture.
C made him friends and enemies.
D was not as good as he claimed.
E was covered in bright colours.
F was left exposed so that people could see it.

Building design

Yes / No / Not Given

❹ <u>Underline</u> the key words in Questions 9–14 and use them to find the right place in the passage. Then read each part of the passage carefully in order to answer the questions.

Questions 9–14

Do the following statements agree with the views of the writer in the reading passage?

Write

YES if the statement agrees with the views of the writer.

NO if the statement contradicts the views of the writer.

NOT GIVEN if it is impossible to say what the writer thinks about this.

9 At first, people were not as enthusiastic about the International Style as Le Corbusier was.

10 The Villa Savoye is an important building.

11 Le Corbusier could have designed buildings that were as big and as impressive as those in New York.

12 Le Corbusier found concrete a difficult material to work with.

13 Le Corbusier's plans for Paris would have ruined the city.

14 Many people show they reject Le Corbusier's style of architecture by living in old houses.

Listening

Note completion

❶ You are going to hear a lecturer giving a talk about a famous structure. Look at Questions 1–10 and decide what sort of information you need for each gap. Match the letters, a–j, with the question numbers.

a the form or appearance of the stadium .....7.....

b a structural part or section of the stadium ....

c what the stadium looks or feels like when you go through the entrance ....

d the number of parts the stadium is divided into ....

e an action ....

f something that comes into the stadium ....

g the number of people who can fit inside ....

h a place to get a good view of the stadium ....

i an amount of money ....

j where the stadium is located ....

Questions 1–10

Complete the notes below.

Write **NO MORE THAN TWO WORDS AND/OR A NUMBER** for each answer.

The Beijing Olympic Stadium

Background details

Inspired by Chinese ceramics.

Consists of **1** .... , which are not physically connected.

Can hold **2** ....

Uses 110,000 tons of steel in its horizontal **3** .... and vertical columns.

Cost **4** $..................

General impressions

Ideally seen from a **5** .... to get an idea of shape and size.

Built on a **6** .... to emphasise its size.

The stadium is known as the Bird's Nest because of its **7** ....

Gives the impression that it is **8** ....

Inside

People feel like they are entering a **9** .... when they walk into the stadium.

The clear roof panels let in **10** ....

62 Unit 10

② 🎧 Now listen to the recording and answer Questions 1–10. Make sure you do not write more than the specified number of words and/or numbers in each space.

③ Which words in your answers match the following definitions?

1 long, thick pieces of wood, metal or concrete used in a building ....
2 changing position or place ....
3 the amount of space between two people or things ....
4 different from others of the same type in a way that is surprising, interesting or attractive ....
5 the brightness that shines from the sun, fire or electrical equipment ....
6 people who watch an event, sport, etc. ....
7 a raised area of land, smaller than a mountain ....
8 a large area of trees, growing closely together ....
9 buildings or other things which have been built ....
10 the word we use for the number 1,000,000 ....

Vocabulary

Word choice

① Replace the words in bold in the newspaper article with words which have a similar meaning. You will find these words in the grid.

E	W	T	I	M	B	E	R	Q	A	W
N	E	E	R	T	Y	U	C	I	T	O
J	A	P	A	R	T	M	E	N	T	S
O	L	P	A	S	D	F	N	G	R	H
Y	T	E	S	S	E	N	T	I	A	L
A	H	J	K	L	Z	X	R	C	C	V
B	Y	B	N	M	C	R	E	A	T	E
L	Q	A	R	E	A	W	E	R	I	T
E	Y	U	I	O	P	A	S	D	V	F
A	P	P	E	A	R	A	N	C	E	G

New residential development fails to impress.

Report by our architecture correspondent

The town council has described Victory Mansions, the new block of **flats** (1 ....) in the **middle** (2 ..*centre*...) of the town as 'an **important** (3 ....) addition to the town's residential facilities'. Your correspondent was invited to attend the opening ceremony, which promised to be a really **fun** (4 ....) event.

The ceremony itself was a rather downbeat affair. Nobody present was impressed by the building, which didn't look particularly **nice** (5 ....), with its grey concrete façade and rather dated **look** (6 ....). Unfortunately, the initial impression didn't change when we were shown the inside. The rooms were not only small but, thanks to the 'environmentally-friendly sound-proofing' **wood** (7 ....) on the walls, rather dark. The architects had tried to **make** (8 ....) a garden **place** (9 ....) on the roof, but it was so small that it could probably only comfortably accommodate five or six residents at any one time.

All in all, a big disappointment. And with prices starting at £500,000 for a two-room flat, you would have to be very **rich** (10 ....) to even consider living there.

Key vocabulary

② Complete this passage with the words and phrases from the box.

affordable	construct	construction	~~demand~~
design	engineers	foundations	housing
improve	knock down	steel	tower blocks

A few years ago, to satisfy the increasing 1 ..*demand*.. for practical and 2 .... 3 .... in my city, the local government decided the best solution would be to 4 .... a lot of the old terraced houses and build 5 .... in their place. At the same time, they decided to 6 .... the city by replacing many of the old-fashioned brick office blocks with modern 7 .... and glass skyscrapers. At great expense, a team of architects and 8 .... were hired to 9 .... and 10 .... a new residential and business estate, and a huge 11 .... programme began. However, as soon as the 12 .... had been laid, the government suddenly announced there was no more money, and the programme stopped.

Building design 63

Writing

Task 2

1 Read this Writing task and the sample answer which follows it. Do not pay attention to any errors in the answer.

> **Write about the following topic.**
>
> *Some people say that modern buildings are ugly and are ruining our towns and cities, especially when these buildings are very different from those around them. Others say that they add variety and interest.*
>
> *Discuss both these views and give your own opinion.*
>
> **Give reasons for your answer and include any relevant examples from your own knowledge and experience.**
>
> **Write at least 250 words.**

Sample answer

When a major new building goes up in an urban area two groups of people usually come forward to give their oppinion about it. One group are positive. They say that it is original and adds intrest to the area. The other group are negative. They say that it is ugly and spoils the area. I live in an old university city. Many of the buildings there are almost 600 years old. Recently a new sience block was built for the university. It was made of concrete it was covered in black glass, and it was taller than the older buildings surounding it. A lot of people hate it, and I am one of them. However I believe that this is a matter of personel taste. What looks good to some people looks terible to others. It also depends on the building itself. A modern building can be very different from those around it but it may actually complement those buildings. For example in the 1980s, a glass pyramid was built in the courtyard of the Louvre muzeum in Paris. It made a lot of local people very angry. They argued that it was wrong to build such a modern structur next to such an old building. In my opinion however, it is visually exciting and actually complements the buildings around it. Many visitors to the city feel the same way, and today it is one of the city's most famos sights. In conclusion I beleive that some modern buildings can ruin a town, but it depends partly on personal taste, and partly on the building itself. As the English expression goes 'One man's meat is another man's poison.'

(279 words)

2 <u>Underline</u> *Yes* or *No* in Questions 1–7.

In the sample answer on the left,

1. has the writer discussed both views? Yes / No
2. has the writer given an opinion? Yes / No
3. has the writer given reasons for his / her answers? Yes / No
4. has the writer included relevant examples from his / her own knowledge and experience? Yes / No
5. has the writer included an introduction and a conclusion? Yes / No
6. has the writer written enough? Yes / No
7. has the writer divided his / her answer into paragraphs? Yes / No

3 Decide where the paragraph breaks should come in the sample answer. There should be *five* paragraphs. Put a slash (/) where the breaks should come.

4 The sample answer contains ten spelling mistakes. It is also missing ten commas. <u>Underline</u> the incorrectly spelt words in the answer, and write their correct spellings below. Then insert the commas into the answer.

opinion ....
....
....
....

▶ Student's Book page 129

5 Now write your answer to the following Writing task. You should write at least 250 words.

> **Write about the following topic.**
>
> *Some people say that living in a high-rise apartment block is a lonely experience because there is no community spirit. Others say that people who live in high-rise apartments have a much better sense of community than those who live in houses.*
>
> *Discuss both these views and give your own opinion.*
>
> **Give reasons for your answer and include any relevant examples from your own knowledge or experience.**

Grammar
Modal verbs

1 Match 1–6 with a–f to make complete sentences.

1 You don't have to walk
2 You have to make
3 I can't afford
4 Can I make
5 You can find
6 Do we have to pay

a an effort if you want to find somewhere to live in this city.
b a deposit when we rent an apartment?
c lots of interesting books on architecture in the library.
d changes to my house without permission from the local council?
e to live here because house prices are so expensive.
f very far in the city to see some really ugly modern architecture.

2 Complete these sentences with the modal verbs from the box, depending on the function of each verb at the end of the sentences. You can use more than one verb in some sentences.

can	can't	could	couldn't	don't have to
had to	have to	may	might	must
mustn't	should			

1 I .... start looking for somewhere to live as soon as possible. (*I think this is a good idea or is important.*)
2 I .... hand in my essay on town planning until Friday. (*It is not necessary for me to do this.*)
3 I .... come round to your place now if you like. (*I am able to do this.*)
4 There's so much crime in the area that I .... keep my doors locked all the time. (*I think this is necessary or essential.*)
5 The council has told me that I .... make any changes to the front of my house without permission. (*I am not allowed to do this.*)
6 When I looked out of the window, the only thing I .... see was miles and miles of identical housing. (*I was able to do this.*)
7 I .... look for somewhere new to live next year. (*This is possible, now, or in the future, but I am not sure if I'll do it.*)
8 I .... understand why so many people dislike modern architecture. (*I am not able to do this.*)
9 I .... call you because I was too busy. (*I was not able to do this.*)
10 Last week I .... give a talk on the architect Le Corbusier. (*It was necessary for me to do this.*)

3 Read this summary of a conversation between Sam and Chris. Then listen to the conversation. Complete the passage which follows it with the correct form of the words and phrases in the box in Exercise 2.

Chris **1** *couldn't* go to Teresa's party on Saturday because he **2** .... finish an essay and start work on an assignment. He **3** .... get the assignment finished by this Friday. He **4** .... hand it in until Monday, but he's going away for the weekend with Pat. He's not sure where he'll go, but he **5** .... drive down to Chichester to see some friends (although before he goes, he **6** .... replace a tyre on his car). Unfortunately, he's not getting on very well with the assignment. He **7** .... find any books in the library, so he **8** .... look on the Internet. He found a website called Unipedia, but his friend Sam says that he **9** .... believe what he reads on that website because it's full of mistakes. Chris wants to know if Sam **10** .... recommend something else. Sam thinks that Chris **11** .... look on a website called Urban Environment. Chris wants to know if he **12** .... sign up or have a password.

Building design

Recording scripts

Unit 1

Track 02
Narrator: One
Woman: Have you moved into your new house yet?
Man: Not yet. But we've got a date.
W: When's that?
M: Two weeks today, on Friday the 13th.
N: Two
W: Have you come far today?
M: No, just from Crawford.
W: Dorford? Where's that?
M: No, Crawford. That's C-R-A-W-F-O-R-D.
N: Three
W: What's your phone number?
M: Do you want my home number or my mobile?
W: You'd better give me your mobile.
M: OK, it's 0870 292720.
N: Four
M: Do you know Sue's address? I want to send her a birthday card.
W: Sure, it's 70 Sidney Avenue, Lowestoft.
M: 17, Sidney Avenue, thanks.
W: No, 70. And that's Sidney with an I, not a Y: S-I-D-N-E-Y.

Track 03
Narrator: One
Man: What's your name?
Woman: Julienne Bailey.
M: Did you say Juliet?
W: No, Julienne. J-U-L-I-E-N-N-E.
M: And Bailey with an i?
W: That's right. B-A-I-L-E-Y.
N: Two
M: I tried calling you last night, but I couldn't get through.
W: Oh, sorry, I was out. Next time, try my mobile.
M: What's the number?
W: Got a pen? OK, it's 0865 701158.
N: Three
W: Could you give me your address, please?
M: Sure, it's 113 Evenlode Road, Fenton.
W: 113 Evenlode Road. Er, could you spell the name of the road for me?
M: Sure, it's E-V-E-N-L-O-D-E.
W: Thanks.
N: Four
M: How long have you been here?
W: Let me see, I arrived on the 1st, no, sorry, I arrived on the 3rd of April, so I've been here for nine days.

Track 04
Man: Hello. Good Moves Accommodation Agency. Ben speaking. How can I help?
Woman: Good morning. I'm calling about an apartment on your website, and was wondering if I could have some more information.
M: Certainly. Can I take your details before we get started?
W: Sure.
M: Right, what's your name, please?
W: OK, my name is Clarice Willard. Clarice is C-L-A-R-I-C-E. And Willard, W-I-L-L-A-R-D.
M: And have you got a contact number?
W: Yes, I'll give you my mobile, which is 0192 8734566.
M: That's great, thanks. And can I ask how you found us?
W: Of course. A family member used you last year and recommended you. So, I had a look at your website and, well, that's why I'm calling now.
M: OK, so, which property are you interested in?
W: The apartment on Statham Street, the one on the 3rd floor.
M: Let me see. Ah, I'm afraid that flat's no longer available.
W: No?
M: No, it went this morning. It's in a really popular part of town. We do have a house on the same street, if you're interested. It's £950 a month.
W: Er, no, I think that's much too expensive. I think an apartment is all we can afford.
M: Oh, so it's not just for you?
W: No, me and a friend. We're both starting work in the town next month.
M: Oh right, so it's two of you. So, let's see. Do you have any preferences in terms of location?
W: Both our jobs are in the town centre, so it would be good to be within walking distance of that, or perhaps a short bus journey away. Neither of us have a car, so we'd be relying on public transport.
M: And what's your budget?
W: I'm sorry?
M: How much can you pay a month?
W: Let me see, er, £700 a month is probably our limit.
M: Each?

Complete IELTS

W: No, that would be for the both of us. We wouldn't be able to pay more than £350 each. Oh, and that would have to include bills. Not phone bills, obviously, but things like electricity, gas and water.

M: Hmm, OK, well, we do have a place in the Bampton district, which is about ten minutes by bus from town. It's a two-bedroom apartment, and it's less than your budget, at £600 a month. Bills would be extra, unfortunately, but that should still work out at less than £700. Although remember that electricity and gas prices are going up all the time, so I can't guarantee that.

W: Do you have an address?

M: I do. The apartment number is 3, and it's at 57 Thorney Leys Road …

W: Hang on, let me just make a note of that. 57 …

M: Thorney Leys Road. Thorney is T–H–O–R–N–E–Y and Leys is L–E–Y–S. And the district is called Bampton. Do you have an email address?

W: Yes.

M: In that case, I can send you the details, and then you can think about it. And if you're interested, I could arrange for a visit so you can see the place for yourself. How does that sound?

W: Oh, that would be really helpful. It's clarice_willard@…..[fade]

Unit 2

Track 05

Narrator: A
Speaker: Do you have a contact number?
N: B
S: How far do you travel to work?
N: C
S: How do you get to work?
N: D
S: Have you got any hobbies or interests?
N: E
S: What do you do?
N: F
S: Can I have your second name, please?
N: G
S: When were you born?
N: H
S: Where do you live?

Track 06

Interviewer: Can I have your second name, please?
Toby: Sure, it's Walliams. That's W-A-L-L-I-A-M-S.
I: Where do you live?
T: 37 Beech Street, Wokingham. Beech is B-E-E-C-H.
I: When were you born?
T: On the 5th of April, 1984.

I: Do you have a contact number?
T: Sure. It's 0529 865 2411.
I: What's your job?
T: I'm a shop manager.
I: How far do you travel from your house to your place of work?
T: 12 kilometres.
I: How do you get there?
T: I usually take the bus.
I: Have you got any hobbies or interests?
T: Oh yes, I like cooking, cycling and travel.

Track 07

Bridget: Hello, Eddie? It's Bridget.
Eddie: Oh hi, Bridget.
B: Listen, Eddie, are you still free to do an article for the college magazine?
E: Sure, is there anything in particular you'd like me to write about?
B: Well, the next issue is about people's lives, you know, people who have done something interesting or exciting. Anyway, I've got someone lined up, and I was wondering if you could interview them and then write the article.
E: All right, that's fine with me.
B: Great. Have you got a pen?
E: Yes.
B: OK, take this down. His name is Tom Coogan.
E: Tom …?
B: Coogan. That's C–O–O–G–A–N. Got that?
E: Sure, and what does he do?
B: He's a travel writer.
E: I don't think I've heard of him. What else can you tell me about him? How old is he? What's he written? That sort of thing.
B: OK, he's 42 years old, er, and he's written ten or twelve books. Let me just check that. Uh huh, twelve books, including his latest. Oh, and he also presents a travel programme on TV.
E: All right.
B: Now, his latest book is about a journey he made across the Gobi desert on horseback. It took him six months, apparently. Anyway, I think he'd like to talk about that, so make sure you ask lots of questions.
E: Fine, I'd better look at a copy. What's it called?
B: It's called *Has Anyone Seen My Horse?* I've got a copy here which I can lend you.
E: OK, and why does he want to talk about that book in particular?
B: It's just won him an award.
E: Really? What kind?
B: Travel Book of the Year.
E: Oh, wow, that's pretty impressive.

B: Exactly, so like I say, ask lots of questions about it. Now, I've arranged for you to meet him on 21st October. That's two weeks on Friday, is that OK?

E: It should be. Have you got a time for that?

B: Not yet, he wants you to call him beforehand to arrange that. I'll give you his contact number. It's 0722, no, hang on, it's 0772 9214490.

E: 0772 9214490. And where am I supposed to meet him?

B: He's suggested his place, which is good as it's not far from the college. It's 138 Lonsdale Avenue, Summertown. Lonsdale is L-O-N-S-D-A-L-E.

E: Yeah, I think I know where Lonsdale Avenue is. You did say 138, didn't you?

B: Right. Oh, and I suggest that you take a look at his website as well. It's got loads of information, so you might want to ask him about some of his other trips. It's at www.tomcooganbooks.com.

E: All right. Thanks for that. I'll let you know how I get on.

B: Great. Thanks, Eddie. Good luck.

Unit 3

Track 08

Hello, everyone, and welcome aboard the Sunshine Express on our journey from London to Naples. I'm Jane Sharpe, the train manager, and I hope you'll all enjoy the trip.

Before we depart, I'd like to tell you a bit about the train and its facilities. Now, we're here on the observation deck, which is where you'll probably spend most of your trip, as it offers the best views, and directly below us is a, well, we call it our leisure centre. There are some games machines, a television, a small library and so on. If you've brought a laptop or computer with you, you can also get onto the Internet here, as it has full wi-fi capability. There's also a small bar where you can get tea, coffee and light meals. For lunch and dinner, you'll use the restaurant car, which is at the front of the train. You'll have breakfast in your cabins, by the way, which will be brought to you by your steward.

The two cars behind the restaurant are where you'll find the second-class cabins. Each cabin has seats which are changed into beds at night. You'll also find a simple basin for washing, and a small fold-down table. First-class passengers, your cabins are at the back of the train. To get to them, you'll need to pass through the lounge. This can be used by everyone during the day, but is exclusive to first-class passengers after 6 p.m.

Right at the back of the train, basically as far as you can go, is my office. If anyone needs to see me, though, please use the phone in your cabin rather than coming to the office. Just press one and you'll get me. If I'm not there, tell your steward you need to see the manager, and he or she will look for me.

Track 09

Right, let me give you a bit more information about the trip. The first part of our journey is from London to Paris, going through the Channel Tunnel. It will take us just over an hour to get to the Tunnel, including a short stop before we get there to pick up some more passengers. From there, it'll be another three hours to Paris, so we're looking at four hours altogether, give or take a few minutes.

A quick bit of advice about passports. You won't need these until we get to the Italian border, so I suggest you keep them in the safe which you'll find in your cabin. Ask your steward – that's the person in charge of your carriage – for a key. That way, you won't need to carry them with you all the time.

Now, meals. As I said earlier, breakfast tomorrow morning will be in your cabins, and this will be served at about 7.30, 7.45, so you'll be able to enjoy it as we travel along the southern French coast. Lunch is at 1 o'clock in the restaurant car, and dinner is at 8 o'clock, although we'd like you all to be at your table about fifteen minutes earlier, at a quarter to, if you could.

When we get to the Italian border tomorrow morning, our train will change engines, and we'll also be getting a new crew. We'll be taking advantage of the stop to have a look around. I've arranged a visit to the local market, a museum and a castle. This will take about four hours, with a break for coffee in a local café, and we'll be back on the train in time for lunch.

A few quick rules. Some of you might have brought your own food or drink on board. That's fine, but could we ask that you consume it in your cabins and not in the restaurant or lounge? Could we also ask you to make sure your cabin windows are closed when you're not in your cabin? And whatever you do, don't get off the train until we reach the Italian border. Apart from the border and one or two other places, which I'll tell you about, any stops we make will only be for a few minutes. I'd hate to leave anyone behind.

All right, so, moving on from the Italian border, we'll be heading… [fade]

Unit 4

Track 10

Researcher: Hello, Joe, good to see you again.

Joe: Hi, you too.

R: So how did you get on with the devices we asked you to test for us?

J: Oh, fine. Well, mostly.

R: OK, well, we'll come back to those in a minute. First of all, I was wondering if I could ask you a few questions about your attitude to new electrical products. This will help us with future marketing. Is that OK?

J: Sure.

R: OK. First of all, how much do you spend on electronic items a month?

J: Hmm, let me see. I don't earn a lot, so I don't have much left after I've paid for things like rent, bills, food and so on. Anything else is a luxury. So, I'd guess about 5%, maybe 10% of my monthly salary.

R: All right, and what influences you in your choice of product? Say you wanted a new mobile phone, how would you decide which one to buy?

J: Well, first I look at reviews on the Internet, you know, what other customers think about them. Then I'll ask my friends what they think. In fact, their opinions are probably more important than anything.

R: How much does advertising help you choose a product?

J: I think that depends on how the product is advertised, and who is advertising it.

R: For example?

J: Well, if it's someone I respect, you know, like a <u>famous</u> sportsman or actor, that can certainly make a difference. I know it shouldn't really, but it does.

R: And where do you buy most of these products? The High Street? The Internet?

J: Most people seem to avoid <u>shops</u>, these days, don't they, for things like that? They think they can get things cheaper on the Internet.

R: Right.

J: But I find that if you say to a shop assistant that you can get a new, er, camera for example, for £100 on the Internet, they'll often match the price. So, that's where I go.

R: Any other advantages?

J: Well, you get personal service and you don't have to wait for the product to be delivered. <u>Ordering</u> online means you have to wait, sometimes for ages, to get the things you've just bought. I hate that. I guess I'm just very impatient.

R: OK, one final question. Do you ever see a product and think 'I've *absolutely* got to get one of those'?

J: Oh, all the time, especially if I'm walking past a shop and I see a new electronic item in the window, especially if it's unusual, you know, something I've never seen before. It takes a lot of willpower …

Track 11

Researcher: Right, Joe, let's move on. Now, we gave you three items to test for us. Let's start with the mobile phone.

Joe: OK, well, it has its good points and its bad points. The purple and silver make it quite eye-catching, you know, modern, exciting.

R: Right. Anything else?

J: Well, it's very small, isn't it? I know people say small is good, but in this case I think you might have gone too far.

R: In what way?

J: It can be a bit difficult to use, especially if you've got big hands like mine. You press one key, and you end up pressing another at the same time. On the other hand, thanks to the oval design, it does fit comfortably in your hand. Mobiles are usually sort of rectangular, aren't they? I think this is much better.

R: OK.

J: What else? When I was sending text messages, I had real problems seeing what I was writing. It's not that the screen was too small, just that it was a bit dark. If you're outside, you can hardly see anything on it.

R: We added a few things that you don't get on other mobiles. What did you think about those?

J: Ah, right, well, that noise it makes if you move away from it? That's really annoying. It's basically a good idea, but I think that after a while it would drive me mad.

R: So, you probably wouldn't buy it?

J: Probably not. When I buy a mobile phone, I don't want one that's going to be difficult to operate. There's no point having a phone that looks good if you have to spend ages trying to make a call or send a text message. It's funny, but I find that more expensive mobile phones are more difficult to use than cheaper ones. It should be the other way round.

R: So keep it simple, right?

J: Right. And I want a phone that doesn't have problems picking up a signal, or doesn't cut you off halfway through a call. And all those games and other things you get on a mobile? I really can't see the point in those.

R: Fair point. Next, the digital radio. What did you think?

J: The audio quality was crisp and clear, even if you turned it up really loud. Some sound systems can sound a bit distorted at higher volumes, but not on this one. So 10 out of 10 for that.

R: Great.

J: The thing is, I'm not sure if it's the area I live in, but the choice of radio stations seemed very limited. It didn't make any difference what I did with the aerial or where I put the radio, high up on a shelf, low down on the floor. And there seemed to be a delay when you turned up the volume.

R: What do you mean?

J: Well, when you press the volume control, for example, nothing seems to happen for a few seconds. And the same thing happens when you want to change radio stations.

R: OK, the third item was the laptop computer. What's your opinion on that?

J: Oh, I really liked it. It's so small, so compact, but easy to use at the same time. I don't think you could make it smaller if you tried. But at £900, I'm not sure you'd get many customers. That's a lot of money for a laptop. Bring that down to, say, £400 and things might be different.

R: Any other changes you'd make? Like adding more memory, for example?

J: I think that's fine as it is. Three hundred gigabytes of memory is probably more than enough for most people. Oh, and incidentally, the way the keyboard folds out so that it's like a full-size one? That's really clever. But the computer doesn't have anywhere you can play CD-ROMS. And I'd include a light in the keyboard so you can use it when it's dark.

R: Well, thanks, Joe, for your comments. I think we …[fade]

Unit 5

Track 12

Hello, everyone, and welcome to our college Natural History day. You've all got your programme for the day, but let me just give you a bit of information about your options for this morning's sessions, which begin at half past nine. Remember, you need to attend one of these sessions.

All right, your first choice is called 'Dogs might fly', which will take place in Room 27. Professor Keenan, who you may remember ran a workshop last year on how dinosaurs became extinct, will be giving a lecture on the evolution of animals. In particular, she'll be looking at how they may evolve in the future, and this will be followed by a group discussion where you'll get a chance to ask her questions and offer your own thoughts and opinions on this. So, if the evolution of animals is something you're interested in, head for Room 27.

We all know that animals communicate with each other, but what about flowers? Your second choice is a video presentation called 'Flowers talk'. This considers the possibility that plants and flowers *do* actually communicate with each other. The video is presented by Patrick Bell, who has just written a book on how plants adapt to their natural environment, so it should be very interesting. That will take place in the lecture room, no sorry, correct that, here in the main hall. We've had to move it because the lecture room is being renovated.

The third choice is ideal for those of you who want to get a bit of fresh air. We've called it 'A world in your garden', which we thought was appropriate as it looks at the sort of things you can find just by stepping out of your front door. Anyway, for those of you interested in getting away from the classroom, Doctor Watkins will be taking you on a nature walk through the local park, and will be telling you about some of the fascinating animals and plants that live and grow nearby. And it's a lovely day for a walk!

The final option, well, you might want to avoid this one if you're frightened of things like snakes, as this is a hands-on workshop where you'll actually get a chance to handle these exotic creatures. It won't just be snakes, however. I believe Tom Howard, our resident reptile expert, has brought some other reptiles along for you to meet, including his pet tortoise, Reggie, who is over 100 years old, and a pet lizard he calls Arthur. So, if you want to meet Reggie and his other reptile friends, head on over to the Biology lab at 9.30. I'm sure you'll have a lot of fun. For those of you who don't usually use the Biology lab, could I remind you that you need to put on one of the white coats by the door before you go in.

OK, now, we've got some students here from Bardwell College who …[fade]

Track 13

OK, now, we've got some students here from Bardwell College who have joined us for today's events. Hello to you all, and welcome.

Now, before our day begins, you'll need to get a guest badge, which you'll have to wear while you're on the college premises. You can get these from the administration office. To get there from the main hall, leave the hall by the door opposite reception, turn left, and just follow the corridor to the end. The administration office is on your right. Don't go any further, or you'll be in the sports hall. If you show your guest badge in the café, by the way, you'll get a 20% discount on drinks and sandwiches. To get there from the main hall, walk along the corridor between the main hall and reception and turn right. The café is through the first door on your left. Directly opposite the café, on the same corridor, is the student common room, where you can go to relax and perhaps meet some of our own students.

If you have any valuables that you don't want to carry around with you, I suggest you put these in a locker. These are next to the sports hall, opposite the administration office. You can get a key for a locker when you get your guest badge from the administration office. And if you want to use our library, leave the main hall by the door *opposite* the one you came in – that's the door by the bicycle parking area – and walk to the end of the corridor. The library is through the door straight ahead of you.

Unit 6

Track 14

Amy: Hey, Matt, are you coming out tonight?

Matt: I'd love to, Amy, thanks, but I've got too much work. I need to get this psychology assignment in by Thursday.

A: Oh, what's it on?

M: Happiness, or specifically, the things that make people happy.

A: Wow, that's a big area. How are you approaching it?

M: Well, I've been looking on the Internet to see what various experts have to say on the subject.

A: Did you find anything interesting?

M: Well, yes, I did.

A: Like?

M: Like, for example, there's a professor at Nottingham University, a guy called Richard Tunney, and he suggests that the more close friends we have, the happier we are. And if you see these friends regularly, go out with them and so on, well, that's even better.

A: I'd have thought that was fairly obvious.

M: I guess so. The next one is a bit more interesting, though. Martin Seligman, a professor of psychology at an American university, conducted a happiness experiment with his students.

A: What did he do? Give everyone huge amounts of cash and then see how much they smiled? That would help, wouldn't it?

M: Well, perhaps it would. For a short while, anyway. No, what he did was tell half his students to take part in fun activities, like playing video games or going to the cinema, and the other half to do good things.

A: Good things?

M: You know, like visiting elderly people at a care home, or some other kind of voluntary work. And it was those students who reported a more lasting feeling of happiness.

A: That's interesting.

M: Then there's George Vaillant, a psychiatrist and professor at Harvard Medical School. He's spent the past 60 years studying people.

A: So, I guess he probably knows a bit about them.

M: He certainly does. According to him, the thing that really makes people happy is having something to aim for, you know, a goal in the future.

A: Right, so I can say 'By the time I'm 30, I'm going to be a millionaire.' and that will make me happy.

M: Ah, but Vaillant has a warning here. You need to be realistic. It's no good setting yourself impossible goals, because, well …

A: Because you'll only make yourself unhappy trying to achieve them.

M: Exactly.

A: So, does anyone mention anything that people *normally* assume brings happiness? Like a healthy bank account, or an expensive house, something more, er, material?

M: Funnily enough, those things aren't mentioned much. Here's another interesting one, though. Melanie Hodgson, she's a professor at Westbrook University, claims that people are happier when they're getting ready to go on holiday.

A: Oh, I love that. Sitting on a beach, relaxing, sightseeing….

M: No, not the actual holiday itself, which professor Hodgson says can sometimes be quite stressful …

A: That's true, they can.

M: … but the things you do leading up to it. Deciding what you're going to take with you, what you're going to see and do, packing your case, that kind of thing.

A: I get it. Yes, I can see how that would work.

Track 15

Matt: I've also found one of those personality tests on the Internet. You know, answer these questions to find out how happy you are.

Amy: Oh, those. They're a bit of a waste of time, aren't they? I did one on 'How healthy are you?' and the results were completely wrong.

M: But they're quite good fun though, aren't they?

A: Well, yes, especially if you do them with friends. I think it's important that you shouldn't take them seriously, though.

M: That's true.

A: Anyway, why should I do a test that tells me how happy or healthy or successful I am? I mean, I already know the answers, don't I? So, I'm not likely to get any surprises, like, oh, according to this test I'm happy – I didn't expect that!

M: OK, I take your point. So what makes *you* happy?

A: Oh, I don't know. Spending time with people I know and like, I guess. I need people around me.

M: Me too. But I need time on my own, as well.

A: That doesn't really bother me. I grew up in a big family, so I'm used to someone always being in the room. If I wanted to be alone, to get away from people, I had to go out for a walk or something. I still do that occasionally. In fact, that's one thing that makes me happy. A long walk in the countryside. And the advantage is that you're getting some exercise too, which is something I don't usually do.

M: But you go running, don't you?

A: Sometimes, but only because I feel I have to. Anyway, back to your assignment. You've got all the information you need …

M: Not quite. I need to do a bit more research first.

A: OK, so you'll be off to the library, then?

M: I would if I knew I could find something useful, but you know how disorganised it is there. It's impossible to find what you want, especially when it comes to psychology books.

A: Oh, I know.

M: No, give me a computer and the Internet any day.

A: Well, good luck with that. If you get bored and want a break, you know where to find me.

M: Thanks, but if I don't get this done, I'll be in trouble.

A: Why don't you email Tony? He did a similar assignment last year, so he might have a few suggestions.

M: That's a good idea. Have you got his email address?

A: Sure, give me a moment while I look it up.

M: Thanks.

Unit 7

Track 16

Advisor: Good morning. International Book Fair ticket office. How can I help?

Caller: Oh, hello, I'd like to book some tickets for the fair, please. And I have a few questions about the event as well, if that's OK.

A: Certainly. Well, let's deal with the tickets first. Er, can I just take your details first?

C: Sure.

A: Let's start with your name and address.

C: OK, it's Wallace. Angus Wallace.

A: Could you spell your surname for me, please?

C: Of course. It's W-A-L-L-A-C-E.

A: Sorry, was that one L or two?

C: Two, er, double L.

A: Thanks, and your address?

C: OK, that's 14 Rose Hill …

A: 14, Rose Hill. Is that 'rose', like the flower?

C: That's right, and it's in Wallington.

A: Oh, I know Wallington. It's just outside Oxford, isn't it?

C: That's right. And the postcode is OX13 3NJ.

A: OX30, 3MJ

C: No, *OX13*, and it's N for November, not M for Mike.

A: Sorry. OX13 3NJ. Thank you. Do you have a contact number?

C: I do. It's 0872 344 9162.

A: 0872 344 9162.

C: Right. That's my home number. If I'm not in, I can be contacted at work, on 0872 298 1191. I'm usually there from 9 in the morning until 5.30 in the evening.

A: And how many tickets would you like?

C: Two, please. For the Saturday.

A: Two for Saturday May 7th.

C: That's right.

Track 17

Caller: How will you send the tickets?

Advisor: I can give you a couple of options. The first is by email, but of course you'll need to print them out yourself. Alternatively, there's 24 Hour Speedmail.

C: What's that?

A: Well, we send them to you by mail, and you'll get them the next day. We'll also send you a text message to your mobile to let you know they're on their way.

C: I think I'll go for that option.

A: Fine. Now, you had some questions?

C: Yes, I understand that there are some talks being given by authors. There's one in particular I'd like to go to, by the novelist Sandra Harrington. Do you know what she'll be talking about?

A: Well, she's got a new novel which just came out, so she'll be talking about that, and will probably read a few bits from it. She'll also be answering some questions about the book she wrote last year, er, I can't remember what it was called …

C: *Fire and Eagles?*

A: That's the one. You'll probably remember she got into a bit of trouble because some people said she had copied another writer's ideas. So, it should be quite interesting.

C: And do I need to book a place in advance if I want to go to one of the talks?

A: You do, yes. You need tickets, and you can only get them in advance, by filling in a form on our website. You then pick them up from the ticket office when you arrive at the fair. We'll send you more information about the talks when we send you your tickets for the fair itself.

C: How much are they?

A: Oh, nothing, they're free.

C: Great, thanks. And what's the best way of getting to the fair from the city centre?

A: Are you driving?

C: Probably not, what with the way the traffic is these days.

A: Well, Duke's Court underground station is only a minute's walk away. Does that help?

C: I'm only a short walk from a station at my end, so that's probably my best option. OK, one last question. Is there anywhere to eat at the fair?

A: Oh, there are lots of cafés and restaurants there. They're generally OK, but unless you're prepared to spend a fortune on a sandwich and a cold drink, I'd go somewhere else.

C: Such as?

A: Well, you'll be much better off going to one of the cafés or restaurants in the streets nearby. Don't tell anyone I said that, though.

C: I won't! Thanks. So, how should I pay for …

Unit 8

Track 18

Hello, everyone. In a few minutes we'll be setting off on our trip to the Palace of Kom Ombane. There are a few things I should mention before we go, so please pay careful attention.

Now, there are three groups of us on this trip, and we'll be using three coaches to get to and from the palace. They each have numbers on the front, and ours is <u>coach 2</u>. Please check that you board the right one, both at this end and when we come back, otherwise I'll be running around looking for you. So, coach 2.

The palace is probably going to be very busy, so please stay close to me when we get there. If you lose me, head for the <u>main gate</u> which is opposite the ticket office, and you'll find me there. Alternatively, call me on my mobile. The number's in your information pack. Your pack also contains a card called a <u>Freedom Key</u>. Keep hold of this, as you can use it to get money off in the cafés and restaurant at the palace.

Now, these days, the palace is a museum, but you'll be surprised to hear that people still live there. No, they're not kings or queens but local people who work at the palace, and their families. Many of them wear traditional clothes, so they make a great subject for a <u>photograph</u>. But please ask them if it's OK before doing this. These people may also offer to sell you small wooden and stone statues that they've made. They make lovely souvenirs. They'll probably ask you for about $20 or so for these, but it's perfectly acceptable – indeed, it's usually expected - to offer them less. <u>30 percent</u> below the asking price would be an acceptable figure, but please don't try to go lower than that. The statues, by the way, are a copy of the large statue of King Hupugarta which is just inside the main gate. A quick word of warning. This is of great significance to the locals, and while nobody will object to you photographing it, they don't like people <u>touching</u> it. So, hands firmly in pockets when you walk past him, please.

OK, so that's the boring stuff out of the way. Does anyone have any questions about …

Track 19

I'd like to briefly tell you about a few of the main attractions at the palace. You'll find these on the map in your information pack.

Now, one of the first things you'll see is the statue of King Hupugarta which I just mentioned. This is on the right-hand side of <u>Monument</u> Court, the main square inside the palace grounds, er, Monument Court so called because of the many statues of kings, queens and other historical figures there. Dating back to 123 BCE, the king's statue is 6 metres high, made of stone with a layer of <u>gold</u>, and dotted with jewels. That's genuine gold, by the way, not just paint. Unfortunately, the jewels are made of glass. The originals were stolen many centuries ago.

Just beyond the court is the Temple of the Sun. This is the oldest part of the palace, and is estimated to be about 2,700 years old. It originally had a roof, but now there are just the columns that supported it. There are 130 of them altogether, each one rising between 20 and 25 metres from the ground to support a frame of iron bars on which the roof originally rested.

To the left of the Temple of the Sun is the New Palace, and it's here that you'll find the Royal Chambers. Er, it's called the New Palace because it's the newest part of the palace complex, although it was actually completed in 1346, which makes it quite old, really. Anyway, the Royal Chambers were where kings and queens from the middle of the 14th century had their private rooms, bedrooms, bathrooms, things like that. It was also where they would have kept all their valuables, although these have now been moved to the palace museum, which is also worth a visit. This was opened in March 2010, no sorry, 2011. As well as valuables like jewellery and other historical objects, the museum also houses an impressive collection of weapons, including a sword that is said to have belonged to King Hupugarta himself.

Unit 9

Track 20

Tutor: Hello, Jo. Come in and take a seat. I wanted to talk to you about your essay on weather control.

Student: Right. What did you think?

T: Well, let's start by looking at your introduction. You say that global warming is causing extreme weather conditions around the world.

S: That's right, isn't it?

T: Well, you need to be careful here. Yes, there is a lot of evidence that this is the case, but the issue is still controversial. You need to specify that many experts *believe* this is the case, rather than saying, 'This is how it is.'

S: OK.

T: Then you look at the issues surrounding extreme weather, er, and how it has a negative effect in some countries.

S: I was worried that that section was a bit disorganised.

T: No, not at all. It's very good, but I was slightly surprised when, in the same paragraph, you mentioned an *advantage* of extreme weather.

S: Not the right place for it?

T: Not really, no. In fact, I would question the need to put it there at all. At one point you're talking about droughts, hurricanes, floods, etc., and then suddenly you're talking about people being able to sunbathe on the beach in January.

S: Ah, I see what you mean. I think I was going to elaborate on that, add more information, but I guess I forgot to do so.

T: OK, then there's the section on weather-control programmes. This made interesting reading, but your ideas didn't really lead on from each other. Did you write a plan before you did this?

S: Er, no.

T: Well, you really ought to. Here's an example. You talk about experiments to control hurricanes, then you write about rain-making experiments, and then for no apparent reason, you go back to talking about hurricane control.

S: So, a bit messy?

T: A bit, yes. Next, you go on to talk about something called 'cloud seeding'. Great, you gave a good, clear explanation about what cloud seeding is, that it's a way of using science and chemistry to make clouds produce rain, and you give some examples of where it's been used.

S: So, that section's all right?

T: Ah, well, listen to this. 'The chemical silver nitrate is introduced into clouds to encourage them to produce rain.' Silver *nitrate?*

S: Oh, that was careless. I meant silver *iodide*.

T: Exactly, I would hate to think what might happen if you started firing silver nitrate into clouds. OK, finally, the conclusion.

S: I always have problems with the conclusion. I never really know what to say.

T: Well, you summarise your main points and give a few opinions, which is great, but you then start talking about environmental systems. This was not only in the wrong place, but I couldn't see where it fitted in with the rest of the essay generally.

S: Right. So, there's a bit of room for improvement, then.

Track 21

Tutor: All right, let's go back to the section in your essay on cloud seeding. Apart from your silver nitrate / silver iodide mistake, you've missed a few bits out.

Student: Have I?

T: I'm afraid so. What I'd like you to do is talk me through the process of cloud seeding, what it involves and so on, and I'll stop you if you've forgotten something. OK?

S: Fine. Well, first of all silver nitr, er, *iodide* is fired into the cloud from the ground using a rocket.

T: Good, and you could mention that sometimes it's dropped from above by aircraft.

S: Right, and this is the first stage, the primary stage, which is called static seeding. The silver iodide causes a chemical reaction with the tiny water drops in the cloud, and they freeze.

T: OK, so you've got millions of tiny ice particles because the water droplets in the cloud freeze. What happens next?

S: Next, er, there's a process called riming. R-I-M-I-N-G. That's when the ice particles, well, they join up to form bigger pieces of ice, and when they're heavy enough, they fall from the sky.

T: Good, and then?

S: Well, as they fall, they turn to rain or snow. And, er, well, that's it, isn't it?

T: Well, usually, yes, but you've mentioned that there's a first stage, a primary stage, so surely you should have mentioned …?

S: Oh, the secondary stage.

T: Which is known as?

S: Dynamic seeding, of course, how could I have left that bit out? Let me think. OK, so the water droplets turn to ice, and, er …

T: What happens when water freezes? When anything freezes, for that matter. Something that may seem surprising.

S: Oh, of course, it releases heat.

T: Exactly, it releases heat. And what can happen to a cloud when freezing water inside it does this?

Recording scripts 73

S: The cloud gets bigger, and contains even more moisture.

T: Exactly, and not only do they become bigger, but they also …?

S: They, er, produce storms. No, hang on, that's not right. They last longer, that's it.

T: Right. They last longer, which means they can be seeded again to produce even more rain.

Unit 10

Track 22

Good morning, everyone. Today, as part of our 21st century architecture series, I'm going to tell you a bit about a remarkable structure which I'm sure you're all familiar with, the stadium that was built for the 2008 Olympics in Beijing.

OK, let's start with a few background details. The stadium was designed by Herzog and de Meuron, a firm of architects from Switzerland. They studied Chinese ceramics, er, plates, cups and bowls, to get inspiration. The stadium is actually two structures, which are completely separate from each other. In the middle there's the seating area, which was originally designed for 100,000 spectators, but this had to be reduced to 90,000. Around this area is the frame, which is made of 110,000 tons of steel in horizontal beams and vertical columns. The architects wanted the roof to open and close, but they changed it because it could have been dangerous if there was an earthquake. The big advantage of changing it was that it reduced the cost by several million dollars, although the building still came to an incredible $423 million.

So, what makes this stadium such an amazing building? Let's start with the general impression it creates. For this, the best place to look at it is from a distance. Why from a distance? Well, that's where you'll really get an impression of what it looks like and how big it is. You'll also notice how it really stands out in its surroundings. This is not just because of its size – and it is big – but also because it stands on a low hill which helps make it higher than any other buildings in the area. Then there's its unusual shape, which has helped to give it its nickname of the Bird's Nest. The unusual shape of the stadium also does something else. You see, if you stare at it for long enough, you also get the impression that this structure isn't standing still, that it's moving in different directions, almost like it's a living, breathing creature. This is especially true at night, when the stadium is lit up from inside with lights that continually change colour.

In the stadium, everything changes. There are visitor entrances all around the outside, and as you enter, you get the impression that you're walking into a forest, and not just any forest, but something magical from a children's story. As you cross towards the spectator area, coloured light comes through the clear roof panels, creating strange pools of light and shadow. Now you're no longer in a forest, but on a set that's been built for a fantasy film. It really is a remarkable experience, and it's only once you're inside the spectator area that you finally realise you're in a sports stadium.

Track 23

Sam: Hi, Chris, I didn't see you at Teresa's party on Saturday.

Chris: Oh hi, Sam. No, I had too much to do. I had an essay to finish for Professor Kearney, and then I started work on my assignment.

S: Oh, what's it on?

C: Modernist architecture. And I've only got until this Friday to finish it.

S: By Friday? That doesn't leave you much time.

C: Well, actually, it's due in next Monday, but I'm going away for the weekend with Pat.

S: Where are you going?

C: Well, we're not sure at the moment. We're thinking of driving down to Chichester to see Mark and Penny.

S: I thought your car was off the road.

C: Well, one of the tyres isn't in very good condition, so that needs replacing, but otherwise it's fine.

S: OK, so how are you getting on with the assignment?

C: Not great, really. I went to the library to look for some books, but there was nothing useful there. Most of the books on the subject had already been borrowed.

S: What about the Internet? Have you tried looking there?

C: Of course. I didn't have any choice. It was that or nothing.

S: And any luck?

C: I found some good stuff on that online encyclopedia, you know, Unipedia.

S: Don't believe anything you read on Unipedia.

C: Why not?

S: Well, it's full of mistakes.

C: Is there anything else you suggest I look at?

S: Try looking at the Urban Environment website instead. It's much better. There's loads of good material there, and it's accurate.

C: Thanks, I'll try that. Does the website ask you to sign up or enter a password to get onto the site?

S: No, nothing like that.

Acknowledgements

The authors and publishers acknowledge the following sources of copyright material and are grateful for the permissions granted. While every effort has been made, it has not always been possible to identify the sources of all the material used, or to trace all copyright holders. If any omissions are brought to our notice, we will be happy to include the appropriate acknowledgements on reprinting.

Text

Text on p. 24 adapted from http://itthing.com/monopoly-game-history;

Text on pp. 25–26 adapted from http://www.ideafinder.com/history/inventions/ballpen.htm;

Colleen & Keith Bragg for the text on pp. 30–31, adapted from http://www.honeybadger.com. Copyright © Colleen & Keith Bragg, www.honeybadger.com. Reprinted with permission;

Childrenslit.com for the text on p. 44 adapted from http://www.childrenslit.com/childrenslit/mai_graphic_novels.html. Copyright © www.childrenslit.com. Reprinted with permission;

The Independent for the text on p. 55 adapted from 'Weather modification: the rain makers' by Rob Sharp, *The Independent* 30.4.08. Copyright © The Independent.

Photos

The publishers are grateful to the following for permission to reproduce photographic material:

p.6A: bumihills/Shutterstock.com; p.6B: Jon Arnold Images Ltd/Alamy; p.6C: Paul Banton/Shutterstock.com; p.6D: wildarrow/Shutterstock.com; p.6E: Jupiterimages/Thinkstock; p.7: istockphoto/Thinkstock; p.8: Ian Dagnall/Alamy; p.10: javarman/Shutterstock; p.13: david gregs/Alamy; p.16: Topham Picturepoint/TopFoto.co.uk; p.21: TopFoto/TopFoto.co.uk; p.24: dreamypix/Alamy; p.25: Topham/Topham Picturepoint/Press Association Images; p.26: Société BIC; p.28A: istockphoto/Thinkstock; p.28B: Christian Delbert/Shutterstock; p.28C: Hemera/Thinkstock; p.28D: istockphoto/Thinkstock; p.28E: Photos.com/Thinkstock; p.28F: Fred Fokkelman/Shutterstock; p.28G: istockphoto/Thinkstock; p.28H: Hemera/Thinkstock; p.28I: istockphoto/Thinkstock; p.28J: Photodisc/Thinkstock; p.28K: R-O-M-A/Shutterstock; p.30: Rob Francis/Shutterstock; p.34R: Norbert Wu/Science Faction/Corbis; p.34L: Ian Scott/Shutterstock; p.35: Ammit/Shutterstock; p.39: istockphoto/Thinkstock; p.42: Arco Images GmbH/Alamy; p.47: Martin Williams/Alamy; p.48: Susanna Bennett/Alamy; p.50: Justin Kase zsixz/Alamy; p.60R: Adam Eastland Art + Architecture/Alamy; p.60L: o2 Architectural Photography/Alamy; p.62: Sergiu Turcanu/Alamy.

Illustrations

Andrew Painter pp. 15, 18, 20L, 54, 58, 59;
David Whamond pp. 36, 51, 63;
Gary Wing pp. 8, 12, 19, 31, 38, 43
Martin Saunders pp. 20R, 32;
Wild Apple Design pp. 10, 11, 22, 34, 45, 46, 47

Corpus

Development of this publication has made use of the Cambridge English Corpus (CEC). The CEC is a computer database of contemporary spoken and written English, which currently stands at over one billion words. It includes British English, American English and other varieties of English. It also includes the Cambridge Learner Corpus, developed in collaboration with the University of Cambridge ESOL Examinations. Cambridge University Press has built up the CEC to provide evidence about language use that helps to produce better language teaching materials.

The publishers are grateful to the following contributors:

Judith Greet: editorial work

Kevin Doherty: proofreader

John Green: audio producer

Tim Woolf: audio editor

Design and page layout: Wild Apple Design Ltd

Audio recorded at: ID Studios, London